NEW DIRECTIONS FOR ADULT AND CONTINUING EDUCATION

Susan Imel, *Ohio State University*
EDITOR-IN-CHIEF

⬧ **W9-DCY-637**

Enhancing Creativity in Adult and Continuing Education: Innovative Approaches, Methods, and Ideas

Paul Jay Edelson
State University of New York, Stony Brook

Patricia L. Malone
State University of New York, Stony Brook

EDITORS

Number 81, Spring 1999

JOSSEY-BASS PUBLISHERS
San Francisco

Enhancing Creativity in Adult and Continuing Education:
Innovative Approaches, Methods, and Ideas
Paul Jay Edelson, Patricia L. Malone (eds.)
New Directions for Adult and Continuing Education, no. 81
Susan Imel, Editor-in-Chief

Copyright © 1999 by Jossey-Bass Inc., Publishers, 350 Sansome Street, San Francisco, CA, 94104.

Microfilm copies of issues and articles are available in 16mm and 35mm, as well as microfiche in 105mm, through University Microfilms Inc., 300 North Zeeb Road, Ann Arbor, Michigan 48106–1346.

ISSN 1052–2891   ISBN 0–7879–1169–0

New Directions for Adult and Continuing Education is part of The Jossey-Bass Higher and Adult Education Series and is published quarterly by Jossey-Bass Inc., Publishers, 350 Sansome Street, San Francisco, California 94104–1342. Periodicals postage paid at San Francisco, California, and at additional mailing offices. Postmaster: Send address changes to New Directions for Adult and Continuing Education, Jossey-Bass Inc., Publishers, 350 Sansome Street, San Francisco, California 94104–1342.

Subscriptions cost $54.00 for individuals and $90.00 for institutions, agencies, and libraries.

Editorial correspondence should be sent to the Editor-in-Chief, Susan Imel, ERIC/ACVE, 1900 Kenny Road, Columbus, Ohio 43210–1090. E-mail: imel.1@osu.edu.

Cover photograph by Wernher Krutein/PHOTOVAULT © 1990.

Jossey-Bass Web address: http://www.josseybass.com

Printed in the United States of America on acid-free recycled paper containing 100 percent recovered waste paper, of which at least 20 percent is postconsumer waste.

Contents

EDITORS' NOTES

There is a renewed interest in human creativity as a focus of interdisciplinary scholarship. Whereas much previous research and writing approached this subject from the perspective of psychology and tended to view creativity as a trait unevenly distributed throughout the population, newer approaches emphasize the role of environment, social organization, and ways of encouraging more creative behavior. For example, a systems approach to creativity encourages us to look at how social environments can be altered to promote creativity. The implications of these new perspectives on human creativity for adult educators are many and far-reaching, extending to the schoolroom, the corporation, and the community, and including enhanced creativity within continuing education itself. The purpose of this source book, then, is to provide adult educators with updated views on creativity and how it can become an essential quality of their professional and personal lives. Unlocking greater creativity in the classroom and in other dimensions of continuing education stands before us as a significant challenge toward which we can strive with both imagination and motivation.

In the first chapter, one of us, Paul Jay Edelson, sets the stage by presenting an overview of current creativity research and its implications for adult education. In Chapter Two, Susan Anderson describes an innovative, school-based peer education model for alcohol and drug prevention. Enhancing citizenship and fostering community change is the topic addressed in Chapter Three by Catherine Flavin-McDonald and Molly Holme Barrett with Paul Aicher and Martha McCoy. They speak from the unique perspective of what a small foundation can do in creatively tackling giant national issues. In Chapter Four, Folkert Haanstra of the University of Amsterdam provides an international perspective through his research on the Dutch creativity centers, whose goal has been to stimulate creativity throughout the Netherlands.

Chapters Five through Eight address creativity in higher education. In Chapter Five, Clifford Baden of the Harvard Graduate School of Education analyzes the development of the world-famous Harvard Institute for the Management of Lifelong Education (MLE). In Chapter Six, Bill Clutter addresses how the strategic direction of a major urban university was changed with the assistance of creative continuing education leadership. In Chapter Seven, James F. Polo, Louise M. Rotchford, and Paula M. Setteducati of Nassau Community College (Long Island) write about a unique partnership with the Bell Atlantic Corporation. And in Chapter Eight, Mary Lindenstein Walshok shows how continuing educators can initiate innovative educational collaborations and have far-ranging impact on their regional economies. We conclude in Chapter Nine with some observations on creativity in adult and continuing education and what we think the major challenges are for the future.

In preparing this volume, we have striven to present examples of original responses to pressing needs. In some cases, as at Harvard, the University of California at San Diego, and in the Bellmore (Long Island) School District, new models for continuing education were developed. In other situations (Nassau Community College, Pace University), creative leadership took on daunting challenges that compelled unique solutions. In every circumstance described, however, continuing educators found it necessary to reach into reservoirs of imagination and commitment in order to achieve important results. We hope this book will serve as both an inspiration and practical guide for our colleagues worldwide as they grapple with creating a future favorable for the continuation of our species with opportunity for all.

We would like to thank Susan Imel, NDACE editor in chief, for her support of this theme; our contributing authors for their patience and cooperation; our School of Professional Development colleagues for their innovation and experimentation; and our respective families for supplying a nurturing environment so essential to our own creativity and growth. It would have been impossible to put this volume together without their collective help.

Paul Jay Edelson
Patricia L. Malone
Editors

PAUL JAY EDELSON is dean and PATRICIA L. MALONE is director of corporate partnerships at the School of Professional Development, State University of New York at Stony Brook.

How can adult education continually adapt to changing social,
institutional, and cultural circumstances? Findings in the area of
creativity research can help us promote creativity among
administrators, faculty, and students as a way of meeting and
defining important emerging future needs.

Creativity and Adult Education

Paul Jay Edelson

Discussions of creativity in adult and continuing education often tend to
become discussions of marketing or program development because these two
sectors are overtly creative in the sense of the new products fashioned—
whether advertising campaigns and materials or courses and programs. Moreover, marketing as a field has traditionally been a haven for "creative" people
who can devise attention-grabbing ads that may even take on lives of their
own. In adult education program development, a similar premium has always
been placed on "coming up with new ideas" for courses, seminars, and workshops. And the people drawn to programming have had to develop a sixth
sense for spotting new adult education trends that are on the upswing and
therefore likely to attract students.

The discussion and review of marketing and new program concepts is the
backbone of many, if not most, continuing education conferences where professionals in our field gather. This is as it should be considering the market-
driven, consumer-driven nature of adult learning in the United States, which
is largely self-financed by voluntary learners who enjoy considerable freedom
of choice in program and institutional selection. This pattern is also becoming
normative worldwide. Without creative marketing and program development,
most continuing education bureaus would simply close up shop, because there
is rarely a central institutional mechanism for the recruitment and allocation
of part-time students in continuing education divisions that are subunits of
larger organizations. In other words, continuing education offices have no one
to count on but themselves. In addition, the steady stream of new programs
keeps continuing education fresh and responsive to changing learner needs.

In this volume and especially in this chapter, we have the unique opportunity to focus on broader meanings and applications of *creativity* in adult

New Directions for Adult and Continuing Education, no. 81, Spring 1999 © Jossey-Bass Publishers

education other than just in marketing or program development, although those areas will be addressed as well. We need to look at creativity in a broader sense—as a resource and skill that we can nurture and enhance for ourselves and for others and as a way of helping our field address new and emerging challenges. Perhaps even more significantly, creativity can help us frame new problems worthy of solving.

Creativity Research and Analytical Frameworks

Scientific research and writing on creativity has been documented since the sixteenth century. Albert Rothenberg, who himself has made valuable contributions to this literature (1979, 1990), cited 9,968 titles for the period running from 1966 to 1974 (1979, p. 7), and certainly this number has swelled even more since his 1979 study. What is it about creativity that elicits so much curiosity? Above all, people recognize that this trait makes possible the most sublime human achievements, adding value to life and to living itself. In art, science, human organization, and every single field of endeavor, the ability to innovate and add value is the driving force of our species. Without creativity we would cease to exist. And even if we could exist, what kind of life would we have?

The coupling of *innovation* with *value* as the key qualities of creativity raise it beyond mere *novelty*, which is synonymous with newness. Not just doing or thinking the impossible, creative ideas are surprising in a "deep way" (Boden, 1990, p. 2). They are an essential ingredient in the evolution of humankind, helping us continually to adapt and solve new problems even if in so doing we generate other, unforeseen predicaments for future generations of creators. Boden makes the distinction between creativity in the personal psychological sphere, or *P-creativity*, which has value for the individual, and *H-creativity*, or historical creativity, which has a profound impact on an age or an era, changing the way an entire culture views and understands phenomena. Thus, a person may be creative at home or at work or through a hobby and have negligible impact on the world at large. Although we will not rule out H-creativity as a realm of creativity that is potentially within our grasp—especially for prolific P-creative individuals—for the purposes of this book we will deal with creativity that is more localized. Yet, if we were to pause and consider the example of using the Internet for adult education, this is truly a creative innovation from within our profession that is reshaping the world. Examples of other adult education creations that have had a deepening impact on the field of education include portfolio evaluation, evening and weekend scheduling, women's programs, corporate outreach, summer school, correspondence and other forms of distance education, compressed fast-track programs, a focus on the learner's need to apply knowledge, and the concept of lifelong learning itself. Whether these were creations of a series of individuals or of teams working together is beside the point. In fact, group creativity is a comparatively neglected dimension of creativity research. But for those of us working in organizational environments, it is germane to consider how teams working together can become more creative, and that is an important theme of this book. Taking a liberty with Boden's schema, presented earlier, we can conceive of *I-creativity*, or interpersonal creativity, denoting the type of creativity that emerges in group processes and especially within organizations.

Great Men and Women Creators. Writings on creativity have often taken the "great man" or "great woman" approach in an attempt to identify core creativity behaviors and traits for emulation. Although informative and interesting, writing about creative geniuses has tended to glorify the extraordinary accomplishments of the relatively few and driven a wedge against the larger mass of humanity. For the amateur artist or inventor, to be constantly reminded of a Michelangelo or an Edison can be a disincentive because few of us—especially as adults—can think of achieving in the remainder of our lifetimes what these and other exceptional men and women accomplished. Even as didactic lessons for schoolchildren, the historical and cultural distances between "great" individuals and ourselves are immense and not easily replicated. Moreover, could we in good conscience advise our children to drop out of school, even if doing so worked for Bill Gates? In addition, writing from the perspective of individual case studies has drawn attention to the bizarre and idiosyncratic and furthered stereotypical images of creative people as either impractical dreamers or mad scientists. From the days when I was growing up, I recall Walt Disney's befuddled cartoon character Gyro Gearloose, not to mention the scores of inventors featured in Saturday matinee horror films who were trying to take over the world with some evil death ray or a mutant army— sometimes both in the same movie. And as mentioned earlier, because more and more of us work closely with others in organizations, it is important to think about how our institutions can provide opportunities for creative teamwork and I-creativity.

Some Useful Generalizations. Nevertheless, the biographical approach, which is often highly psychoanalytical, has yielded useful generalizations about creativity. For a review, see Boden (1990), Csikszentmihalyi (1997), Gardner (1993), Rothenberg (1979, 1990), and Wallace and Gruber (1989). For example, we learn that the creative geniuses are obsessively hardworking and sacrifice many other pleasures and activities, including at times relations with other people, for the sake of their overriding passions. As children they often benefitted from supportive family members (parents or close relatives), who spotted their special brilliance at an early stage. Sometimes, even when there were serious setbacks, these outstanding creators persevered in spite of ostracism and ridicule. These creators also benefitted from devoted allies, who at first formed a protective shell around them and later acted as disciples helping to spread the word and gain support. Yet, after reviewing numerous case studies, Csikszentmihalyi observed that the paths to greatness vary and there is no single pattern (1997).

Mastery and Plasticity. A key factor in creativity is the mastery achieved by outstanding creators in their life's work. The combination of personal curiosity, motivation, and ability to persevere over time led to the development of virtuosity and the necessary sense of plasticity within each creator's respective field. Curiosity and drive are what may be called the "yin and yang" of creativity (Csikszentmihalyi, 1997, p. 185). With deep knowledge, experience, and the confidence to experiment comes reshaping perceptions of a field in a new and unanticipated direction for others to follow (or reject). Gardner (1993) discusses the examples of Picasso's co-invention (with Braque) of cubism and Freud's development of the field of psychoanalysis to illustrate the impact of creativity in reshaping entire domains of understanding. Based on his research, Gardner estimated that it took the creative geniuses in his study approximately ten years to master their respective areas before they could make their astounding creative leaps. Boden, Gardner, Csikszentmihalyi, and Rothenberg emphasize repeatedly that these and other examples of world-class creativity emanate from hard work and persistence and are not "gifts from the gods" (Boden, 1994, p. 81) bestowed on certain fortunate individuals. The ability to innovate with value—to perceive a new way of doing things—and the drive to carry the new ideas through to completion come only after the expert knowledge is acquired and mastered.

The DIFI Model. In recent years the psychobiographical approach to creativity has been supplemented by a more contextual and systems-based framework that stresses the interaction between individuals and their social contexts. Frequently referred to as the DIFI model, which stands for Domain-Individual-Field-Interaction Model, this analytical framework compels us to look at *individual* creativity as an outcome of the interaction between a particular *domain* of activity (biology, music, computer technology, and so on) and a group of experts, collectively known as the *field,* who pass judgment on the contributional value of the proposed innovation within the domain. This model helps explain why some creative people die unknown and unappreciated only to be resurrected by experts in a later era. For example, the paintings of Van Gogh, unsalable in his lifetime, now are sold for millions. The creative value attached to his work is now enormous and has increased independently of any additional input from the long-deceased artist. What is different is our era's fascination with the unique vision of a disturbed individual and how psychological perspectives play a central place in the creative arts. For comparable observations concerning creators who were only recognized posthumously (such as Mendel, Copernicus, Mozart, Rembrandt, and Poe), see Rothenberg (1979, p. 6). Gardner also gives the examples of Emily Dickinson, in poetry, and J. S. Bach, in music, as people who were not prized during their lifetimes (1993, p. 40). The DIFI model tends to ask not *who* is creative but *where* and *why* creativity occurs.

Environment and Creativity. The interaction with the environment in enhancing human creativity helps explain why creative individuals will gravitate to certain cities or institutions where they can find positive reinforcement from others who are working in the same domain. The outstanding individuals examined by Gardner in *Creating Minds* (1993) all found themselves attracted to the major metropolises of North America or Europe. Paris, St. Petersburg, Berlin, London, New York, Vienna—all were remarkable cultural centers, filled with excitement and anticipation of the future. Within these cities talented individuals often formed circles of like-minded creators. Dube's research (1985) on the German expressionists details the myriad urban groupings and regroupings of these artists in Berlin, Munich, and other cities as they explored the meanings of modernism at the turn of this century. Referring to New York in the decades following World War II, Tomkins (1995, p. 117) observed "the kind of group synergy . . . that once pulled first-rate pictures out of second-rate abstract expressionists." This phenomenon is very similar to the "assembly bonus effect" noted by Bass (1990, pp. 611, 621) to account for the increased productivity individuals experience within high-performing organizations.

For adult educators the positive contribution of environment to creativity is a very significant line of thought because it can lead to an examination of educational and work settings and how they can influence human behavior. John Kao's book *Jamming* (1996) explores business creativity and how attention to working space—physically and interactionally—improves creativity. Whimsical places where colleagues can meet, sit down, and exchange information— "playgrounds" and "playpens" (p. 67)—can help to establish the necessary psychic space where staff members can do their best creative brainstorming. Csikszentmihalyi (1997) discusses a number of general ways in which human environments can be made more conducive to creativity. These include incorporating unusual and beautiful surroundings, using furnishings and accoutrements that reinforce individuality and uniqueness, and "personalizing patterns of action" to help focus attention on "matters that count" (p. 145).

Creativity, Self-Efficacy, and Adult Education

The more generalized view of creativity is of a capability that we all have to varying degrees (Boden, 1990). Moreover, Gardner observes that there is no "absolute divide" (1997, p. 5) between the ordinary and the extraordinary; we all harbor within us creative seeds that are capable of flourishing. Even if we cannot become famous creative geniuses, we can still use our creativity to lead more enriched and rewarding lives. In the constant churning of our work, it is easy to lose sight of threads of continuity that transcend the desk, office, and institution. The creativity exercised in any single sphere has the capacity to generate growth in other dimensions as well. Finally, the purposeful concentration needed for mastery—a precondition of focused creativity—can initiate cycles of developmental momentum carrying us to more fulfilling and challenging places.

By believing that we can act creatively in ways that alter our future positively, we exercise and develop our own *self-efficacy,* a concept developed by Bandura (1986, 1997) to explain why some people are able to behave with purpose and confidence to achieve their goals. This coupling of creativity and self-efficacy can produce a remarkable synergy. Having the desire to create, acting on this desire, and using creativity as a means of furthering the attainment of worthwhile objectives can be an effective lever for positive social evolution and global change. This evolutionary optimism is a leitmotif throughout creativity research; in fact, a seminal book by Feldman, Csikszentmihalyi, and Gardner is entitled *Changing the World: A Framework for the Study of Creativity* (1994).

A similar idealistic and utopian plan for the future has been a consistent feature of American adult education since the colonial period (Kett, 1994). As a nation, we have always believed that education, and especially adult education, is a force for both personal and social improvement—to elevate our character, or to help us be more informed and skilled, or to enrich society economically or by enhancing democratic tendencies. Whether this is simply a matter of blind faith or subject to incontrovertible proof, it is nonetheless a cornerstone of the adult educator's creed—that adult education is, without reservation, a positive good. It would be difficult for members of our profession to advance the opposite position—that adults' access to further education should be restricted because of negative personal and social consequences. Of course, problems do arise when discussing financing, priority access, and issues of quality, revealing a more complex landscape of competing needs and values. The need to maintain programs through financial self-sufficiency has also eroded the ability to maintain equal access.

Nevertheless, the conviction that adult education is both additive for the individual and formative for the society at large makes it a prime vehicle for enriching our culture along multiple dimensions. The truism that adult and lifelong learning are now ubiquitous features of our modern technologically driven world means that each year more adults are exposed to some form of continuing education than ever before. Can the development of creativity and acknowledgment of the importance of self-efficacy play a part in curricula across the board? This question repositions creativity as a generic quality and not just a feature of the "creative arts" or continuing education marketing and new program development.

An interactive interpretation of creativity, as in the DIFI model, shows the interdependence of domains, fields, and individuals in engendering what we view as creativity. That is, for the stamp of creativity to be applied to a proposed change, innovations must be validated by contextual application. They must be useful and help to generate additional value. From this analysis, we can see the importance of promoting creativity within an organizational setting. But going further, can we infer from this interactive system that institutional climates may be modified to support creative behavior? Bandura (1986), writing on motivations for creative behavior, notes the importance of both internal and external stimuli. He is not alone in observing that creative people have the compulsion to create, yet not all of them do so to the extent to which they are capable. All of us can quickly recognize that there are times when we ask ourselves "Why bother?" when confronted with challenges in our own environments requiring amelioration. Conversely, there are numerous occasions when we contribute above and beyond what is expected. If we desire colleagues and coworkers to invest the effort to improve institutional aspects of adult education—from faculty development, staff retention, curriculum, student evaluation, placement, administrative processes, counseling, and yes, marketing and program development—what can we do?

Rarely do we look at these issues from the front end, asking how we can improve creativity. More often, we bemoan its absence. Before going further, it is necessary to ask the question of how much creativity we actually desire. Csikszentmihalyi (1997) observed that conditions of too-prolific creativity can swamp the assessment abilities of domain and field, leading to a chaos of unsubstantiated competing innovations. Although our primary focus is on overcoming institutional inertia and stagnation, we are still compelled to seek at some early stage a way of managing innovations so that they can be evaluated for practicality—but without dampening the enthusiasm and motivation of the innovators ("Why bother?"). Change itself is risky, and there is often an uneasy relationship between innovators and the public who question the value of the proposed "improvements." Breaking through this wall of resistance is difficult for both parties!

How Adult Educators Can Promote Creativity

There are a number of significant ways in which adult and continuing educators can act in support of creativity.

Organizing for Innovation. Peter Drucker (1993) recommends the institutional strategy of supporting *puny innovations* as a way to lower the bar for would-be innovators while at the same time minimize institutional start-up costs. He acknowledges several realities—a limited resource base, the fact that change is risky and often rejected—but also notes that change is mandatory for organizational growth and survival. Because Drucker perceives so much institutional energy invested in support of ongoing processes, he doubts that the new can establish roots without adequate support from "top management" or an "executive in charge of innovation" (p. 162). For the larger company he recommends spinning the new project off into a separate business, although this is scarcely possible for the majority of institutions we inhabit, which must be satisfied with managing creativity while also struggling to support routine activities within the uncertain resource base of continuing education. Both Kao and Drucker recommend rigorous monitoring of innovation while at the same time understanding that demanding too quick a return is counterproductive. Drucker observes that it is easy enough to say no and far more difficult to address the requirement of purposeful innovation. We must also ask ourselves, "What is our own future view?" Is it for more of the same? Or do we desire to come closer to achieving the ideals embedded in our field? A vote for a better future compels institutions to support creativity. And doing so helps generate the necessary preconditions for its emergence.

Enhancing Motivation to Create. People are creative for both intrinsic and extrinsic reasons. External incentives may include recognition awards, participation in conferences, and the additional allocation of resources. Edelson (1986) studied the distribution of national continuing education program awards in the United States and found that the frequency of innovative program awards was directly related to continuing education institutional leadership policies that emphasized public recognition of staff for exemplary projects. Helping individuals discover their own values can strengthen the intrinsic motivation to create.

Promoting Self-Efficacy. Bandura (1986) describes the types of behavioral feedback individuals use to shape their own concepts of self-efficacy (pp. 399–406). These sources of information include praise and constructive criticism from second parties, observing others, and monitoring their own performance. Continuing education leaders can increase self-efficacy among staff members in the ways they structure work settings and through their own interaction. This requires behaving in a supportive manner, suspending frequent and unnecessary criticism, and creating opportunities for mastery and professional growth. Bandura notes that developing "collective efficacy" (1986, p. 449) through group behavior can leverage individual accomplishment to still greater heights. He writes insightfully on how the dynamics of organizational life can be modified to support human accomplishment (1997).

Developing Expertise. Developing staff expertise is the most important action leaders can take to enhance creativity in the workplace. This is fundamental to achieving the necessary mastery required for ongoing experimentation within a domain. Professional development then becomes a paramount activity. Individual conferences with staff are an excellent way to communicate the value of continued professional growth and to develop personal expertise plans (PEPs). Individuals perform better in areas of continued practice.

Time for the Generation of New Ideas. Mintzberg (1973) characterizes administrative life as brief, varied, and fragmented. Time is a precious resource for creative people who need some buffering from day-to-day distractions in order to develop new concepts and approaches. A flexible release-time policy that might permit leave, designate certain days as "creative days," and offer latitude in individual work schedules can communicate institutional support for innovation.

Feedback and Reality Checking. New ideas need to be talked through in a supportive yet objective manner. It is important to address the most obvious objections in order to give the creative project a chance of survival. A small-group setting provides both support and the opportunity to suggest modifications as well as standards for assessment. The group can also recommend an initial resource allocation level for the new project.

Playing at Work, Working at Play. There is a close relationship between play and creativity. In play we focus on enjoyment, downplaying long-term goals and focusing on the immediate satisfaction derived from what we are immersed in doing. Both play and creativity are open-ended and generative of new possibilities and combinations. The enthusiasm for play, sometimes captured in group brainstorming, demonstrates that it has the capability for producing creative solutions to long-standing problems (Osborn, 1993). In these and similar situations creativity may profitably be viewed as *intelligence having fun*. The spirit of play demands tolerance for misses and near-misses. Csikszentmihalyi's identification of *flow* (1993) as a feature of creative behavior has much in common with the release and fulfillment found in play. See also Sikorski's book on how to have fun at work (1995).

Personalized Environment. Reinforcing one's individuality through customizing space, equipment, and even the use of time can free one's mind to allow for intense concentration on "matters that count" (Csikszentmihalyi, 1997, p. 145). Csikszentmihalyi emphasizes the importance of transforming the environment so that it is supportive of the individual's own personal creativity rhythms.

Plan for Accidents. The unexpected and unanticipated compel new improvised solutions that often outperform our expectations. The phrase "necessity is the mother of invention" reflects the importance of accident and unplanned circumstance to creativity. Although I do not make an argument for chaos, the need for the unusual and unplanned should cause us to downplay the metaphor of the "well-oiled machine" as an organizational ideal. Even if this were attainable, what creative person would want to work for one?

Staff Selection. One ability that creative people have is to see things from a different perspective. Whether this ability is a cause or effect of their creativity, they may not often fit in or easily conform with prevailing notions of acceptability. Whether rebel, dreamer, or tinkerer, the price an individual pays for creativity is some dissatisfaction with the way things are and the courage to buck the majority viewpoint. When selecting a new staff member we should look for the person who will question and promote change and who is not out of the same mold. Still, new people need nurturing and must gain experience and mastery before they can profitably shake things up. And it would be poor leadership to expect a new hire to go it alone without adequate guidance and support from more experienced colleagues. Hiring staff with different outlooks and skills is a sure way to bring about organizational change. Combining this with strategies to enhance creativity among long-term staff can dramatically regenerate an organization.

Group Interaction. The modern office environment is one of group work addressing complex problems that span individuals and units. Organizational leaders must be able to develop productive and imaginative teams capable of resolving these novel interdepartmental problems. By varying team compositions to reflect divergent viewpoints and encouraging marginal voices, we can bring forth less predictable outcomes and out-of-the-box thinking that our climate of constant change and new technology requires.

Conclusion

The question remains: Creativity toward which goals? We have already alluded to the traditions of adult and continuing education that emphasize access, skills attainment, personal fulfillment, economic competitiveness, citizenship, and social democracy (Elias and Merriam, 1980). Going beyond these broad categories, it is incumbent upon us to work within our own settings to identify significant challenges and opportunities. Whether they are in contract training, workforce development, basic skills, ESL, continuing professional education, or the other varied dimensions of our field, the range of problems is simply too numerous to list and to conceptualize fully. The rapidly changing nature of adult education, which comes in response to worldwide and national trends, means that the need for creativity has never been greater. The study of creativity provides a much-needed infusion of concepts as well as frameworks for the understanding and support of human originality, which can make it possible to address these emergent needs. Through their application we can invigorate ourselves and others and move closer toward fulfilling the ideals of our profession.

References

Bandura, A. *Social Foundations of Thought and Action: A Social Cognitive Theory.* Englewood Cliffs, N.J.: Prentice-Hall, 1986.

Bandura, A. *Self-Efficacy: The Exercise of Control.* New York: Freeman, 1997.

Bass, B. M. *Bass & Stogdill's Handbook of Leadership.* (3rd ed.) New York: Free Press, 1990.

Boden, M. *The Creative Mind: Myths and Mechanisms.* London: Weidenfeld & Nicolson, 1990.

Boden, M. "Creativity: Inspiration, Intuition, or Illusion?" In P. Davies, J. Cobb Jr., S. Boyden, and M. Boden (eds.), *God, Cosmos, Nature, and Creativity.* Edinburgh: Scottish Academic Press, 1994.

Csikszentmihalyi, M. *The Evolving Self: A Psychology for the Third Millennium.* New York: HarperCollins, 1993.

Csikszentmihalyi, M. *Creativity: Flow and the Psychology of Discovery and Invention.* New York: HarperCollins, 1997.

Drucker, P. F. *Innovation and Entrepreneurship.* New York: HarperCollins, 1993.

Dube, W.-D. *The Expressionists.* New York: Thames & Hudson, 1985.

Edelson, P. J. "Creating an Environment for Excellence." Paper presented to the National University Continuing Education Association Region II Conference, State College Pennsylvania, Oct. 16, 1986.

Elias, J. L., and Merriam, S. *Philosophical Foundations of Adult Education.* Malabar, Fla.: Krieger, 1980.

Feldman, D. H., Csikszentmihalyi, M., and Gardner, H. *Changing the World: A Framework for the Study of Creativity.* New York: Praeger, 1994.

Gardner, H. *Creating Minds: An Anatomy of Creativity as Seen Through the Lives of Freud, Einstein, Picasso, Stravinsky, Eliot, Graham, and Gandhi.* New York: Basic Books, 1993.

Gardner, H. *Extraordinary Minds.* New York: Basic Books, 1997.

Kao, J. *Jamming: The Art and Discipline of Business Creativity.* New York: HarperCollins, 1996.

Kett, J. F. *The Pursuit of Knowledge Under Difficulties: From Self-Improvement to Adult Education in America, 1750–1990.* Stanford, Calif.: Stanford University Press, 1994.

Mintzberg, H. *The Nature of Managerial Work.* New York: HarperCollins, 1973.

Osborn, A. F. *Applied Imagination: Principles and Procedures of Creative Problem Solving.* (3rd rev. ed.) Buffalo, N.Y.: Creative Foundation Press, 1993.

Rothenberg, A. *The Emerging Goddess: The Creative Process in Art, Science, and Other Fields.* Chicago: University of Chicago Press, 1979.

Rothenberg, A. *Creativity and Madness: New Findings and Old Stereotypes.* Baltimore, Md.: Johns Hopkins University Press, 1990.

Sikorski, J. *How to Draw a Radish and Other Fun Things to Do at Work.* San Francisco: Chronicle Books, 1995.

Tomkins, C. "London Calling." *The New Yorker,* Dec. 11, 1995, pp. 115–117.

Wallace, D. B., and Gruber, H. (eds.). *Creative People at Work: Twelve Cognitive Case Studies.* New York: Oxford University Press, 1989.

PAUL JAY EDELSON is dean of the School of Professional Development and director of the Professional Development Research Center at the State University of New York at Stony Brook.

*This chapter describes the development of a drug and alcohol prevention
program that is facilitated on a parent-to-parent basis in an elementary
school setting.*

Peer-Facilitated Adult Education

Susan Anderson

The idea of creating a peer model of adult education developed out of a social
worker's need to provide a program of substance abuse prevention within a
school district. Having treated the catastrophic end of family dysfunction for
over ten years in an acute psychiatric service, I wanted to intervene at the earlier stages of family development. The questions that remained were these:
How can I provide a substance abuse program to elementary schoolchildren
that will have long-term effects? How can I integrate a family systems model
within a public education setting? How can I provide a dynamic program that
can promote psychosocial change within the family? How can I send the message of substance abuse prevention and family wellness to the community at
large? And finally, how can I provide these services with limited professional
resources? I was but one family systems specialist for an entire school district.

The Community Parent Center Emerges

After a year of trial and error, the program that emerged in answer to these needs
came to be called the *Community Parent Center.* In its early stages the program
roughly resembled a peer-facilitation model, but there were many stumbling
blocks to overcome before it actually functioned on a parent-to-parent basis. It
was overcoming these stumbling blocks that led to creative program development. The result is a unique model of adult education that is self-sustaining, facilitated by parents, runs on personal growth and development, and even earns
money—both for the parents and for the community.

Many of the novel features of this model grew out of the need to synthesize two seemingly disparate disciplines—psychotherapy and education. The
Community Parent Center evolved as a viable hybrid, a self-generating new

NEW DIRECTIONS FOR ADULT AND CONTINUING EDUCATION, no. 81, Spring 1999 © Jossey-Bass Publishers

species that soon spread beyond its own boundaries and adapted to new environments, bringing its message of substance abuse prevention and family wellness to neighboring communities.

It was possible to bridge the gap between the two models because the goals of the social work profession and those of the educational system are compatible. Both disciplines are interested in promoting competent, sound, healthy individuals and ultimately in enhancing psychosocial evolution, although they differ in how they meet those goals. An elementary school's primary function is to educate, to increase knowledge base, skills, and awareness within the scope of its curriculum. A social worker's primary function within the school is to facilitate change—change at the level of attitude, feelings, and behavior, change that promotes emotional health.

To clarify how educational and psychosocial approaches function differently, let's take smoking prevention as an example. An academic approach to smoking prevention would be to offer information about the facts and statistics related to the dangers of smoking, techniques for quitting, and a database of available resources. In contrast, the social work profession has made a rigorous study of *resistance to change*—the phenomenon that accounts for the fact that in spite of increased awareness about the risks of smoking, many well-informed people continue to smoke. A social worker's program on smoking prevention would make this very resistance the focus of its intervention strategy; its program would be targeted to activities that enable participants to change their behavior. Providing information that "smoking isn't good for you" is one approach; providing a vehicle designed to help people to stop smoking involves a very different focus and methodology.

Targeting Parents. In keeping with the family systems approach, the primary beneficiaries of the program I had in mind were to be the children—but the immediate impact would be on the parents. The program would be designed to help parents change their highly routinized, automatic behavior patterns that interfered in the positive development of their children. An example is parents' tendency to become frustrated and yell at their children. By teaching parents techniques for building children's self-esteem and competency, parents can transfer these skills to their families. Thus, the benefits of the program were to trickle down to the children.

This top-down approach is in keeping with a family systems model that seeks to intervene at the higher-organizing level of the system—in this case, the parents—on behalf of its constituent parts—in this case, the children (Donigian and Lalnati, 1996). The point was to help parents help their children grow into healthy adults.

An analogous paradigm was being integrated within the elementary school district. Instruction was moving away from the mechanistic approach. Using the skill of language as an example, instruction was moving away from the traditional method in which children were taught to build from letters to words, words to sentences, and sentences upward to meaning. The new paradigm in which teachers were being trained guided students first to the overall context and meaning of a targeted subject and then to the composite word-symbols and operational skills. Thus, in view of the theoretical congruence between family systems and holistic educational models, the school climate provided fertile ground for the development of a holistic family systems approach to substance abuse prevention.

My first attempt was to set up family therapy services within the school, but this attempt was doomed to failure. Parents were not comfortable confiding about the intimate details of their personal lives in the all-too-familiar environment of a public school, whose halls still held the echoes of their own childhood memories. I would have to find another way to intervene in the family system.

Developing a program of parenting education workshops seemed to be a more congruent approach, but it was not without its own drawbacks. Parenting education offered an information-based program rather than one promoting psychosocial change. Yet parenting education was more in sync with the overall activity structure of the school and less threatening to parents. In addition, it fit into the school's stated mission *to promote parents-as-partners-in-education.*

The task then was to design a parenting education program that could incorporate psychosocial dynamics. Peer group dynamics is a well-known technology for promoting peer pressure capable of motivating behavioral change (Dryden, 1995; Christner, 1994). Building peer process into the program design would create a vehicle for helping parents change entrenched patterns of behavior. The program would make use of information-based content but its success would not be measured in terms of how much the participants learned cognitively; instead, success would be measured in terms of observable behavior change.

Process Versus Content. Peer interaction creates a learning laboratory in which parents can learn a particular skill—validating feelings, for example—by learning how to validate each other's feelings during the course of the workshop. As they learn its benefits experientially as well as cognitively, the positive peer pressure of the group dynamics motivates them to transfer this enhanced skill to their parent-child relationships.

Thus, the program was to operate on two levels: an educational level involving exposure to *content* information and a *process* level involving peer interaction. The content consisted of the principles of parenting—how to build your child's self-esteem, set realistic expectations, improve behavior, promote achievement, and enhance the parent-child bond. Because these principles involved the acquisition of effective communication skills and other prosocial behaviors, it was clear that the information was ideally suited to a peer group format. Parent-child communication skills mirror adult-adult communication skills. Through parent-to-parent interaction, these principles could be easily modeled, practiced, reinforced, and internalized within the dynamics of peer process.

The Facilitator's Role. The facilitator's role is gradually to transfer control of the group to the participants. As responsibility for group process emerges from within, the highest level of adult functioning in each person is reinforced.

Group Structure. To create the optimal environment in which peer interaction can build, chairs are arranged in a circle, each equidistant from the center, making a structural statement for each member's equal value. The circle provides a contrast to the traditional classroom arrangement in which a teacher stands before rows of students as the expert bestowing information to the less well informed. Members of a circle are able to focus on the group experience rather than on an identified leader. In the traditional model, the leader is expected to serve as the primary source of the information. Once a peer process is established, the interaction, rather than the leader, becomes the primary source of new ideas and skills. The circle allows for a lateral style of communication in which participation is even. The leader becomes a *participant observer,* sitting within the circle side by side with the other members, conveying program information in a conversational rather than a formal manner.

Obstacles to Creating Parent-to-Parent Process

In initiating the first series of parent workshops, there were obstacles to creating the peer dynamics I planned for. The parents' expectations tended to be at odds with the function of a peer group; they expected to receive information the same way their children received it—from a teacher or expert. This expectation for a parallel process caused parents to *look up to* the facilitator as the source of information, thus creating a hierarchical relationship in which they positioned themselves as students—as subordinates—to an expert.

Subordinated in a recipient role, parents had no difficulty attending to the program's content on a cognitive level but were less prone to engage in peer interaction. By focusing on the leader, they were less likely to discover the wisdom of the group or tap into their own capacities for self-education, mastery, and *change.* In other words, in the presence of an identified expert, the group dynamics that I was hoping to facilitate did not materialize.

The techniques for overcoming resistance to group process are well known. For any social work facilitator, the struggle to localize power within the membership is expected to involve a persistent effort (Rosenthal, 1994). But because the parenting education program was set within a school culture, the parents clearly expected the professional advice of an expert. Balancing these expectations with the need to promote peer process became most apparent each week as I presented the didactic portion of the program.

Each workshop began with an open peer discussion about family issues that arose during the week. But this process was disrupted the moment I commenced to present the day's topic. Doing so placed me in the teacher role, causing many parents to lapse into hierarchical positioning once again and begin deferring to me as the expert, asking me questions that would be better answered by the group: "Is it all right to speak?" "How does this technique apply to my situation?"

To overcome this, I began presenting the didactic portion of the program through self-help materials, which included commercially prepackaged audiotapes, videotapes, and workbooks. Asking parents to take turns pushing the *Start* button, I was able to step into the background as these parent-level resources were able to supplant the need for expert or teacher. With information being presented in the form of impartial resources, parents were less prone to subordinate themselves to the learning experience. Instead, they were able to engage the information laterally, through mutual discussion. The parents were invited to critique the self-help materials and determine for themselves whether the information had any useful application to their own family situations. Having truly become consumers of the information rather than mere recipients, parents were in a position to exercise the power of choice; they could assert their individuality and autonomy within the peer process. Through the use of parent-level resources, the parents' highest level of ego functioning was reinforced and honored, and the tendency toward subordination to the expert was minimized.

In spite of the use of the circle and the self-help resources, a constant influx of new members into the program—a desirable occurrence—posed an additional challenge to the process. New parents, expecting to receive straightforward professional advice, tended to overlook the tenuous peer process that was developing and tried to draw me in as teacher, directing expert questions to me and taking the focus off the group process. Because I am a mental health professional, it was natural for them to identify me as teacher or expert in parenting education. The truth was that parenting education was a brand-new technology for me; my area of expertise was helping people access their own innate wisdom, their capacity for self-discovery and change. Because I was learning about many of the precepts of parenting techniques through the same prepackaged materials, I began engaging in a parallel process of learning *with* the parents. By sharing my own struggles in learning to implement these techniques within my own family, I was able to show them that an "expert" can also be a peer.

Benefits of a Peer Group

Although I was able to facilitate information by becoming part of the peer process, the program still had a ways to go before it could serve as a dynamic vehicle for change. As long as an identified professional was present, new parents tended to reinfect the group with expectations for a hierarchical learning process and dilute the peer dynamics. The result was that the practicing behaviors of autonomy and self-directedness between the other group members temporarily declined in response.

My determination did not diminish, however. The peer group process I was aiming for offered many benefits. When members learn that they cannot rely on a leader or expert to make the group meaningful, each begins to take responsibility for the quality of the discussion, for adhering to the format, for following its guidelines, and for maintaining balance, fairness, and purpose. As members take on these responsibilities, their adult functioning levels increase in the context of the group. They gain comfort in the group and begin to risk higher levels of participation, becoming more competent and confident in their abilities. The group builds self-esteem as members experience their positive impact on one another. These behavioral changes represent real gains in personal growth and development, empowering parents to manage better the difficult challenges of raising children.

An additional benefit to group process is that as members feel integral to the group's success, a sense of belonging and group cohesion sets in. Positive peer pressure motivates members to come back each week; parents look forward to having their efforts validated by their peers. And as participants attend over an extended period of time, the parenting principles and substance abuse prevention messages that are the basis of the program's content are reinforced through repetition.

With these goals in mind, I persisted in my efforts to minimize the role of expert and maximize the horizontal process of peer interaction. Yet there was still a tendency for many parents to give me credit for gains that were clearly coming from within themselves. In other words, my identified role as a professional was still interfering with the program's ability to allow parents to gain a real sense of their own abilities.

The implication of this was radical: I would have to remove myself from the process altogether before a pure parent-to-parent model could reach optimal levels. And indeed, it was in absenting myself from the workshops that a creative new model emerged.

Creation of a Leaderless Group: A Pure Peer Model

The break came toward the end of the year. Eight to ten regular attendees had become a cohesive core, showing up for each group regardless of topic or location. Why not teach these core participants to become peer facilitators? Why not provide them with the tools to facilitate their own parenting workshops for other groups of parents? Then I would be able to step back and support the parent education program from a distance and assess whether the program's goal to promote change at the level of the family system was being achieved.

When I first proposed this idea to the core group, they were understandably reluctant. They did not believe they could acquire enough skill to run the workshops. I pointed out that I had been modeling a peer facilitator role all along, that I had been letting the prepackaged materials play the expert role. I explained how the peer model allows greater levels of self-esteem and personal empowerment to develop within the group, rather than allowing all of the credit and esteem to be given to the leader. As parents, they could create a true peer model of facilitation and bring the messages of parent education to other parents on a parent-to-parent basis. My professional status was actually an impediment to that end. As peer parents, they could provide a more effective group process, unencumbered by all that a professional title represents in a school system.

My new focus in program development was to find ways to reassure my prospective trainees of their own capabilities. I reassured them that models for peer-facilitated group programs had been established by Maxwell Jones (1994) with the concept of the *therapeutic community* as well as by the women's consciousness-raising groups that developed in the late 1960s and early 1970s, in which a peer-facilitated format was used successfully, honeycombing the country with leaderless women's groups and creating a revolution of change (Shreve, 1989).

I also emphasized that it was not necessary for them to become expert parents to become parent facilitators. They needed only to learn to follow a simple format and to facilitate the prepackaged parenting materials, the tapes and workbook exercises they were already familiar with.

As we continued to address their many apprehensions and concerns, we found ourselves engaged in an intensive peer dynamics of our own, one that led to a creative process of program development and helped build significant innovations into the program. For instance, in order to feel confident, the peer facilitators needed to see a "how-to"—an easy-to-follow script that would make it possible for them to run successful workshops for other groups of parents. So we developed what we called a *recipe for success,* a written document printed on a three-by-five card that came to be referred to as the *parent-facilitator format.* It served as a basic blueprint, a script that prescribed a sequence of activities designed to make each workshop session proceed smoothly, comfortably, and meaningfully. The next idea was that parents would run the workshops in pairs. Each would have a peer facilitator sitting across from him or her in the circle, helping to follow the script and offering on-site support. The idea of cofacilitation was built into program policy. All parent-facilitated programs were to be run by twos.

The prospective facilitators expressed concern about whether other parents would be interested in attending programs run by nonexperts. Out of this concern came a plan for marketing the parent-to-parent program that involved outreach strategies designed to assess community needs and provide responsive programming on location.

Before launching the first series of parent-facilitated workshops, we tried to anticipate the problems that might come up in the course of running a group. The biggest concerns were these: What if members are silent? What if someone attempts to dominate the group? What if members look to the parent facilitators as experts? What if members begin attacking one another? What if they disagree with the materials being presented? In addressing these concerns, written guidelines for troubleshooting were developed. Also developed were posters that could be openly displayed in the various workshop locations, reinforcing important program policies and disclaimers. For example, one poster read: *Materials being presented do not represent the philosophy of the Community Parent Center but are provided to stimulate discussion. Critique is welcome!*

Another innovation was the development of the weekly peer-facilitator supervision group, which provided ongoing support to parents who were cofacilitating workshops, allowing them to pool experiences, address problems, and help shape overall program direction. As always, I modeled the participant observer role, preparing written materials in advance rather than taking on a teacher role during the supervision group process.

Program Launch

The facilitators were ready to begin outreach to their churches, temples, recreation centers, libraries, children's schools, clubs, and other organizations. They succeeded in drawing parents to attend their first round of workshops. Their programs were successful. Parent facilitators enjoyed their roles, and their new group members responded enthusiastically to the parent-to-parent format.

How then could we continue reaching more parents and allow the program to be ongoing?

A New York State Youth at Risk Community Partnership Grant was obtained to promote the success of the program. It covered the cost of materials, space, secretarial support, technical assistance, and advertising, such as press releases, radio announcements, fliers, guest presenters, and the like.

The money also provided a salary to the peer facilitators in order to compensate them for their time and justify their absence from their families on the many evenings and weekends when they were running workshops. The small stipend averaged about $15 per session, a remuneration that served as a form of external validation.

The grant money inspired a new line of thinking for the parent facilitators. They decided that they would charge a fee for their workshops, with "scholarships" offered for parents who couldn't afford to pay on a confidential-request basis. The facilitators wanted to demonstrate that they were able to earn back their own expenses, and they took pride in the business venture side of the program. Money added a kind of token economy, another element that made the program attractive to the community. Charging for the workshops made a statement attesting to the value of these services.

As more parents from the community began attending parent-facilitated workshops, they wanted to know how they too could become peer facilitators. It was decided that anyone who accrued thirty hours of parenting education workshops would be eligible to be trained as a parent facilitator. The "thirty-hour certificate" provided a powerful incentive for parents to continue attending workshops on an ongoing basis. So intense was attendance that a second tier of trainees was eligible by the end of that first year. Each year there was a new tier of facilitator trainees who were trained *not* by the original trainer but by the previous tier of trained parent facilitators. By now a whole technology of written guidelines and training methods had evolved to support what had become a turnkey training program.

Thus, an achievement ladder was created; facilitator salaries increased according to their tier in the program. Incentives offered for accruing multiple thirty-hour certificates included continuing education units (CEUs), invitations to advanced workshops, assignments to paid positions, and other specialized roles and perks within the program.

An Expanding Model Today

Today, some parent facilitators have been running programs for over ten years. The senior parent facilitators visit other school districts to help set up peer models that adapt to the unique needs of diverse settings. Thus, the peer model of adult education is spreading throughout the neighboring communities, carrying its message of substance abuse prevention and family wellness and increasing parents' confidence and competence along the way.

References

Christner, A. M. *Addiction and Family Systems*. Providence, R.I.: Manisses Communications Group, 1994.

Donigian, J., and Lalnati, J. *Systemic Group Therapy*. Pacific Grove, Calif.: Brooks/Cole, 1996.

Dryden. *Facilitating Client Change in Rational Emotive Behavior Therapy*. London: Singular Publishing Group, 1995.

Jones, M. *The Therapeutic Community*. New York: Basic Books, 1953.

Rosenthal, L. *Resolving Resistance in Group Psychotherapy*. Northvale, N.J.: Aronson, 1994.

Shreve, A. *Women Together, Women Alone: The Legacy of the Consciousness Raising Movement*. New York: Viking Penguin, 1989.

SUSAN ANDERSON is a family systems specialist who provides a substance abuse prevention program in Bellmore School District and has a private practice in Huntington, New York.

The authors interview Paul Aicher, founder of the Topsfield Foundation, Inc., and Martha McCoy, executive director of the Study Circles Resource Center, about the challenges of creating an effective, replicable model for citizen engagement through communitywide study circle programs.

The Topsfield Foundation: Fostering Democratic Community Building Through Face-to-Face Dialogue

Catherine Flavin-McDonald, Molly Holme Barrett

Many foundations are looking for ways to contribute effectively to community-building efforts. One of the biggest challenges for national foundations, as outsiders, is to find a balance between assisting a community and nurturing long-term change that is truly owned and driven by that community. A related challenge is to extract the lessons of successful community building so that effective programs can be replicated throughout the country.

The Topsfield Foundation, Inc. (TFI), an operating foundation based in Pomfret, Connecticut, has been unusually successful in meeting these challenges. In its short life, it has made great strides in reaching the grass roots and making a contribution to the field of democratic community building.

Paul Aicher, Topsfield founder and president, knew he wanted to use the foundation's resources to support grassroots citizen efforts. Through the Study Circles Resource Center (SCRC), TFI has had a real and sustained impact on hundreds of communities, large and small, across the country. Topsfield and SCRC assist cities and towns as they build communitywide study circle programs. In these programs, large numbers of ordinary citizens meet in small, participatory groups to address critical public issues, learn from one another, and find ways to work together.

Paul Aicher's partnership with the Topsfield board and staff is a story of innovation, collaboration, and commitment. Together, they work to support, guide, and learn with a growing network of civic entrepreneurs. In the following interview, Aicher and SCRC Executive Director Martha McCoy reflect

NEW DIRECTIONS FOR ADULT AND CONTINUING EDUCATION, no. 81, Spring 1999 © Jossey-Bass Publishers

on the history and challenges of building a national resource center dedicated to promoting the practice of citizen deliberation.

The Initial Idea and Start-Up

Paul, would you tell us about your vision of the role of philanthropy in helping to build a stronger society? What is its potential?

PAUL: Certainly, the potential is impressive. Philanthropic organizations are easy targets for failing to do the impossible: solve problems on their own. Really, private philanthropy is both praised and vilified: praised when it gives its resources to programs and ideas we believe in; vilified when it's the reverse. Even though regulations limit nonprofits from direct engagement in the political process, almost every project is "political"—even if it is something as nonpartisan as voter registration. The challenges of private philanthropy are many, but so are the opportunities.

Smaller foundations—like start-ups in the for-profit world—can be innovators. Yet innovation in the nonprofit world is quite different. Defining success is much more difficult, as is understanding one's unique role as a funder. That role, I believe, is to be an innovator, to support that which is not yet fundable by the public.

To support real innovation, I suspect that grantmaking foundations are better off when they bet on people and the concept rather than insist on outcomes that aren't definable. You may not really know about the impact your work is having until long after you have spent the time and the money. Certainly, outside analysis is wise, but—just as parents and teachers aren't sure of their effect on a student or child until much later in life—some gambling and trust are necessary.

What would I do if I were king? I would say that foundations should mainly support grantees' core budgets rather than special projects. So many creative organizations are forced to cook up special projects when their real worth is in growing the things they were founded for. That's hard for foundations to do. Program officers naturally want a sense of being creative and, thus, tilt to an organization's "special" stuff rather than fund the core budget. I think we need to understand that new ideas take time to develop and that some organizations in the civil society field need funding for more than the usual three years. The bottom line for me: find good ideas and good people, and give them some time to succeed.

Paul, as a social innovator as well as a funder, how do you contribute to the success of the projects that you begin? Martha, what have you observed about how that combination works?

PAUL: In introductory phases, in the creative periods, project staff commonly are burdened with false expectations. Too often, funders fail to give organizations time to evolve. In the beginning stages of an organization, it is necessary to develop a clear charter and find ways to creatively use resources to fill that charter. You need to focus your energy on the staff, encourage them to be entrepreneurial and really get out there. You've got to ask them tough questions—be persistent in the Socratic method, I would say—and support their work.

MARTHA: I must add that Paul is anything but a disengaged philanthropist! He works with the SCRC staff on almost every aspect of the project. Of all the things that he brings to the work, probably the most vital are his commitment to service, his sense of urgency, and a thoroughly healthy skepticism. "Are we being as useful as possible to the communities we serve—and to communities that may call us tomorrow?" He's taught us that while it's always possible to fill our time with "good work," that's not enough. He pushes us to ask the hard questions about whether we're working in the smartest, most effective ways to carry out our mission.

PAUL: I certainly try to do that. And it is really important to create an organizational culture where employees are just as disciplined in the nonprofit world as they would be in business. To do otherwise not only wastes resources, but it demoralizes people when they see an exciting opportunity being squandered. Really, the similarities between the for-profit and nonprofit worlds are greater than their differences. You've got to concentrate on finding good people for the organization, having a culture that reinforces creativity, and staying focused.

You can't just ride in on a white horse, with money and ideas, and expect your ideas to hold sway. You have to really listen to the people who have been working in the field all along. Stirring the pot is a good thing to do, but it should be the kind of "pot stirring" that helps people advance their work and helps them question assumptions that may no longer be useful.

Why did you invest your time and resources in advancing small-group deliberation?

PAUL: When I was fresh out of engineering school, I was looking for a way to become better informed on national and global issues. The Fund for Adult Education was just starting at Northwestern University, and I became a participant and later facilitated groups for several years. In structure, they were much the same as present-day study circles—they were small groups that met over four or five sessions, the materials gave a range of choices, and the facilitators were not experts but were trained to keep the discussion on track. Later, in Pennsylvania, I helped found a World Affairs Council, which used the Foreign Policy Association's Great Decisions discussion series. These discussion guides are still produced by FPA, and are wonderful for people who want to talk about issues of global concern.[1]

Later on, following my involvement with groups working on nuclear disarmament, I concluded that most people, regardless of how they came down on the issue, weren't listening to each other. They were simply throwing darts at one another while taking comfort in the justice of their own position. This caused me to think back on my small-group discussion days and to establish the Study Circles Resource Center. I wanted that vision of what could happen in democratic small-group discussion to permeate our ways of getting engaged in critical social and political issues. That's still my long-term vision and belief, that face-to-face work between citizens is highly necessary—and that its value is little understood.

Interestingly, once people actually take part in study circles, they immediately come to see the value and potential of their participation. That's why I knew that our energy and resources had to be used to find ways to bring people out, to help give them this experience. Then they would be committed to making it happen for others.

Paul and Martha, how did the study circle idea fit in with other small-group discussion programs that already existed?

PAUL: The use of small-group discussion as a learning tool is hardly new. A study done at the beginning of the 1990s showed that at least one-third of all adults in America had participated in such programs in a recent five-year period. Many of these programs, such as participatory Bible studies, are based in religious organizations (Wuthnow, 1994).

At the turn of the century in America, the Chautauqua movement was active in thousands of communities throughout America, often using small-group discussion to help people work through public policy concerns. Participatory discussion was also a focus of the Progressive Era—for example, in the Social Centers movement. The Studebaker series, originating in Iowa in the 1930s, was another such program. In the fifties, the Ford Foundation sponsored The Fund for Adult Education, which engaged people in small-group discussions about global issues. As I mentioned, there is a direct line from my participation as a facilitator in this program to the creation of SCRC (Gould, 1961; Mattson, 1998; Burch, 1960; Edelson, 1991).

Today, a glance at the field of small-group discussion reveals several dozen national programs. Some focus on specific places or issues; others, like the Foreign Policy Association's Great Decisions and Kettering Foundation's National Issues Forums, address numerous public policy issues.[2] When we surveyed the field, we believed we could contribute by helping democratic deliberation become more widespread. Many people said there was a real need to find ways to bring people out who wouldn't normally think of themselves as part of the "civic crowd." Others wanted to find out how to apply democratic discussion to the community issues they face on a daily basis, issues that are also directly related to the pressing national issues in our country.

MARTHA: It was also during our early formation that we "discovered" the study circle idea. Study circles had sprung up in this country in the late nineteenth century as a cooperative learning model that helped ordinary people educate themselves. It was an era when formal education was often beyond people's reach. In Sweden, study circles became the backbone of the adult education system (Arvidson, 1990; Kurland, 1982; Oliver, 1987, 1992; Aicher, 1991).

There are several characteristics of nineteenth-century study circles that still apply today. They are small, democratic, and highly participatory. They are ongoing rather than limited to one meeting. Participation is voluntary. And they are led by ordinary citizens who facilitate the discussion instead of "teaching" the group. We thought that those qualities gave the study circle idea great potential for responding to current-day challenges to democratic participation. As a result of all this, the Topsfield Foundation focuses it efforts on helping to build community-based study circle programs around critical social and political issues.

Once you had the idea of small-group discussion as the centerpiece of the Topsfield Foundation's work, how did you proceed to implement the idea?

PAUL: At first, we served as an information clearinghouse and networking agent for those who were considering taking part in deliberative discussions. Within six months, we learned that most of the material available was produced by advocacy groups. Worthy as it was and is, it is not what study circles are about. The basic tenet of study circles is that all points of view are put on the table for discussion. Our discussion materials are rooted in this concept.

In our early days, we experimented with several ideas for expanding the numbers of people who would take part in the discussion of issues. For example, we thought that making the materials brief and more accessible would make it easier for program organizers to bring people out. Well, the materials worked well once people got to the discussion, but they didn't really help with the organizing challenge. Once again, we began phoning and visiting, talking with people who were in communities. How did they see small-group discussion as helping them address the issues of their communities? And how would it help them meet their own organization's mission? At this critical time in the organization's development, Martha came onboard.

Martha, how did the early staff work to implement Paul's vision?

MARTHA: By 1993, we knew that for the study circle concept to be viable as a commonly used process, we had to find a new way to bring people into study circles. The concept and materials were clearly workable within the context of the small group itself, but getting a broad participation—one that was representative of a whole community—required a new approach. This was an organizing question: What would bring people to the table?

Around that time, there were two significant trends in the country that influenced the decisions we made about our work. One was the rising importance of the issue of race. Even before the 1992 disturbances in Los Angeles, community people from all over the country expressed a desire to bring people together around the issue of race. After what happened in Los Angeles, that desire was heightened. Second, increased attention to "community building" was starting to happen at both the national and the community level. People were beginning to name something that has since blossomed in countless ways—for example, with the Alliance for National Renewal, spearheaded by John Gardner and the National Civic League, and in the National Community Building Network, inspired by Angela Blackwell. And some public officials at the national level—such as Senator Bill Bradley—were taking active leadership to strengthen our civic life.

These trends led us to write a study circle guide on race relations. In the expectation that people needed to meet several times to really make progress, we designed a multisession guide that began with a session on personal connections to the issue, then progressed to considering the nature of the broader issue, to considering alternative approaches to addressing it, to finally, "What can we do here?" The basic progression—with some variations—has been used in all our guides since.[3]

The other major difference in the guide was that we asked communities—whole communities, not just organizations within communities—to think about how they could use this material to organize on a broad basis. The guide encouraged them to do so, without specific suggestions as to how that would take place. In 1993, the mayor of Lima, Ohio, saw the guide and saw the value of using small-group discussion to help people address racial tension in that city. It was in Lima that the cross-sector model for organizing communitywide study circles first came to be. We worked along with Lima as they figured out how to involve large numbers of people from all across their community, and together we learned so much. They were terrific pioneers! They still are, as they keep figuring out ways to expand the study circle participation in that community. One of the greatest experiences of my life has been watching the transformation of the Lima community (McCoy, 1997; Ashby, 1997).

PAUL: As we have worked with more and more communities, the communitywide study circle model has been amended, adjusted, and refined. It always will be, as different communities make it their own. But the basic idea is rooted in a premise about democracy: that the whole community is the context in which citizen deliberation can be fully meaningful and explicitly connected to community change. While there are other applications of the study circle process (for example, in schools, in the workplace, or in paired congregations or other pairs of organizations), it is the communitywide model that represents the bulk of our effort.

Growing SCRC: Problems, Challenges, and the Messiness of Creativity

While SCRC has remained committed to the idea of small-group discussion, its mission has evolved over time. What have been the most important developments in the mission?

PAUL: At heart, Topsfield and SCRC are motivated by a faith that face-to-face dialogue is a powerful force for social change. We've seen this in study circle programs across the country. We've always worked from a fundamental principle that the impact of the small-group experience extends into other spheres of community and politics. That is, when people get together, delve into discussions about important issues, and begin to feel real ownership of them, they're more likely to go out and become engaged in other aspects of community life and politics. They are profoundly affected by their encounters with other participants, and by seeing connections between their own experiences and big, sometimes abstract, public issues. To create the conditions for this to happen, early on, we focused on the how-to's of creating constructive dialogue—how to build discussion materials, how to train facilitators, those kinds of things. We continue to build on that early work, and the core ideas still hold true.

MARTHA: Absolutely. Over the years, we've learned that people want to make a difference and, when given the opportunity for meaningful participation, they will get involved. We've learned that communities must tie deliberation to opportunities for community problem solving. Also, our discussion guides frame the issues in the broadest possible way, to invite everyone into the conversation. For example, when we created a guide on education, we called it *Education: How Can Schools and Communities Work Together to Meet the Challenge?* And that broad, practical orientation permeates every session. We've helped organizers bring elected officials into study circles—not just as sponsors of the program but as participants in the discussions. We also work with organizers to develop strategies like action forums that invite participants of all backgrounds to work together on solutions to the issues.

PAUL: As you can see, the theoretical links have always been there; now, we're working hard to make them tighter. The mission of getting more people involved as citizens hasn't changed. But our ideas about how to help make that happen have certainly evolved. We know that the trick is for people to view their participation in study circles as something that can be enjoyable and stimulating, not as a duty. That's a challenge. Robert Putnam, in his now-famous article "Bowling Alone," pointed out how Americans have become less active in their communities (Putnam, 1995). TV is most often considered the culprit. As one study circle organizer put it, all you have to do is convince someone to leave their house on a rainy night, go somewhere they aren't sure they can find, talk with people they don't know, on the last night of "Seinfeld!" Always, the challenge is to be sure that the experience is both enjoyable and meaningful.

The "meaningful" part of that equation is probably the most important, more important than we realized at the beginning. That has been the critical part of the evolution of our mission. Many people actually care very deeply about issues—about racial divisions, about their schools, about the young people in their communities—but they don't see how they can do something to make a difference. When the study circles give them a vehicle for deliberation and action, they "fill a hole," something that is missing in the civic life of our communities. And we have seen that large numbers of people, from all walks of life, will get involved when they see that their participation can make a difference. And that's exciting.

What other challenges have you had to address in "growing" SCRC?

MARTHA: Having the right people on staff is, of course, the most critical thing. The challenge is to find capable, dedicated people who have the right blend of skills to help the communities we're assisting. It's hard work, and requires special skills and special leadership. As you might imagine, the pool of people prepared for a career in democratic deliberation on a national scale, community by community, is fairly small. The work requires a lot of travel, the ability to work with communities that are facing critical issues, and the skills to help people work together who may never have worked together before. It requires the ability to communicate the excitement of participatory democracy and its rewards, even though the outcomes in any one community will never be known until the citizens of that community deliberate and create their own results! Members of the staff and our amazing group of field associates constantly inspire me.

The communities we work with are the heart of our network. Nothing would work without those community organizers and their own commitment, hard work, and passion. We try to find ways to support them, partner with them in their learnings, and constantly turn their lessons back out to others in the field. We feel that's the best way we can honor their work—turn it into still more study circle programs around the country.

Since we are a fairly small staff (a total of twelve, including SCRC and Congressional Exchange [CX], SCRC's sister project) working in a big country, our biggest challenge is to understand what it is we do that really makes the difference. There are so many choices to be made about how to spend resources that we must constantly assess what is most useful. And there is always the need to think through long-term strategy. There is never a week that goes by that we don't talk about the long-term plan.

SCRC plays an interesting and challenging dual role. On the one hand, it acts as the "national hub" of a process for democratic community building; to play that role, it promotes the message and practice of democratic dialogue, works to develop hands-on tools and a constancy of meaning and quality control, and constantly learns from communities. At the same time, it "gives away" the process, urging communities to make it their own. This is a tension that is inherent in being a catalyst for democratic change. We are always challenged to find the balance between leading and supporting.

What role does creativity play? How would you define creativity at its best?

PAUL: I think it was Woody Allen who said that 90 percent of being successful is showing up. I think he meant the same thing as Thomas Edison when he insisted that the bulk of his creativity was perseverance. The first thing to understand about creativity in the social change field is that you have to understand your purpose. The trick is to know well enough what it is you are trying to do that you are able to separate out the marginal from the truly useful. Most of the time, it isn't really big things but lots of little things that add up.

MARTHA: Creativity is messy! It requires lots of willingness to search for answers, even when we think we're going over the same ground again and again. It means you're willing to take a risk, to fail, and to change course if you need to. That part gets harder the more you have an established reputation and credibility—it seems too risky to try new ideas. But we have tried hard to disseminate the idea that we are learning with communities, that we aren't claiming to have any final answers.

But as Paul said, you have to keep your eye on what it is that you hold most valuable. That channels your creativity, so that it's much more grounded than "let's try this," or "let's try that." One example: because we had a good sense of our end goals, we were able to see how Lima, Ohio, might become a good model for other communities. We kept thinking about all the community groups around the country who were calling us on a daily basis, who were asking, "How do we engage more people in citizen discussions? How do we get them to the table? How do we make it a meaningful experience—one that they will come back to?" We knew that if we couldn't learn real answers to those questions (questions that could be tested in real community settings), we wouldn't be achieving our mission.

What about collaboration? It's talked about a lot, but has it worked for SCRC?

MARTHA: Collaborative relationships generate opportunities for creativity. For example, when Lori Villarosa (a program officer at the C.S. Mott Foundation) saw how study circles were making an impact on racial issues, we worked with her to develop a program to document best practices in communitywide study circles. That program is just getting under way. Some of our most creative moments come from honestly sharing our "learning edge" with people whose learning edges are just a bit different. In the final analysis, being open to examining your best ideas takes something from being so-so to something that is really worth doing.

I'm also very proud that SCRC's staff works collaboratively, very much as a team. That's critical to our success. As director of an organization devoted to democracy building, it would be inconsistent to manage hierarchically. Of course, the buck has to stop somewhere, and we each have our own roles and responsibilities. But in our normal operations, we value and practice inclusive decision making. The staff has a real voice in important decisions and real authority to help shape particular program areas. This in-house collaboration invariably generates ideas and inspires effective teamwork.

What are your measures of success? How do you determine whether you are (or might become) successful in the work you are doing now?

PAUL: I found that to be one of the hardest things in moving from business to philanthropy. Still, I'm not quite comfortable with the premise of your question. You seem to be asking, "Is it worth it?" Of course it is. We see powerful things happening in communities all over the country—in places like Lima, Ohio (Bainter and others, 1998); Wilmington, Delaware (Flavin-McDonald, 1998); Alread, Arkansas; Springfield, Illinois; and Los Angeles, California. The list goes on and on. When you see study circles motivate lots of people to talk to each other and work together in new ways, you know you're making a positive impact (Leighninger, 1997). At the same time, in this kind of endeavor, the bottom line is not always easy to find. There is so much work to be done.

A lot of things tell me we're on the right track. Are study circle programs happening, and what does the demand look like? By all indications, thousands of people across the country have taken part in study circles. Thousands have been trained as facilitators. The impact those people have on their communities is powerful. What they experience in study circles flows outward. And the demand for our services is only increasing.

MARTHA: That's very true. What's more, we will forever ask ourselves, "Are we disseminating a model that a community can really do on its own?" That's our long-term goal. This is critical because we have a finite amount of time, staff, and resources to apply, and it's a big country. We can help, but the work has to come from—and belong to—the community. We constantly strive to improve our program model so that communities can really own it. And we are learning the factors that make successful programs so effective—they are inclusive, cross-sector, deliberative, participatory, and they connect dialogue and action.

Paul, what are the greatest long-term tensions, and where do you see Topsfield's work and study circles heading?

PAUL: I think one of the greatest tensions for those involved with social programs is whether one's efforts have long-range relevance. In social change work, you have to be careful in determining whether the hothouse conditions at the early stages of a project are replicable once you leave, or when conditions change. We need to be sure that what we see as positive signs are not due to fleeting circumstances. Another long-term concern is in doing what you can to ensure that, when you are no longer around, the board or a new president can step in without any loss of momentum.

Another important tension is one that some people see as inherent in democratic leadership. One can provide vision and resources but, over the long term, success comes only when many people are making their own contributions and finding their own solutions. We can't patent study circles, but we can support them and share what we know is important. Only in that way can we achieve our long-term mission of helping communities see grassroots, democratic dialogue as a permanent way of doing their public work.

As for the future of the organization, the best legacy I could hope for would be an organization that takes advantage of opportunities as they arise. I hope that it always has as its first priority a commitment to effective service. And if the organization is choosing between "What if we were to try this?" and "We've always done it this way," I certainly hope it will opt for the former.

Notes

1. Each year, the Foreign Policy Association (FPA) publishes Great Decisions, a series of articles on current foreign policy issues. For information, call FPA at (800) 628-5754; to order, call (800) 477-5836; fax: (212) 481-9275; e-mail: sales@fpa.org. Or visit FPA's Web site at www.fpa.org.
2. National Issues Forums (NIF) publishes issue booklets to aid balanced discussion of public policy alternatives as they relate to important social issues. To inquire about the booklets and other publications and programs, contact NIF, 100 Commons Road, Dayton, Ohio 45459-2777; phone: (800) 433-7834; fax: (937) 439-9804; Web site: www.nifi.org.
3. The Study Circles Resource Center (SCRC) offers discussion guides on a variety of issues, including race and race relations, crime and violence, education, youth issues, immigration, community growth and change, diversity and American pluralism, and neighborhood issues. SCRC also offers how-to publications for organizing and facilitator training. *Focus on Study Circles,* SCRC's quarterly newsletter, chronicles the development of study circle programs and the ideas behind the process. SCRC can help communities organize large-scale, communitywide study circle programs using these materials. For free assistance, contact SCRC, P.O. Box 203, Pomfret, Conn. 06258; phone: (860) 928-2616; fax: (860) 928-3713; e-mail: scrc@neca.com. Congressional Exchange (CX), a sister project of SCRC, seeks to provide new ways of bringing citizens and members of Congress together in direct deliberative dialogue about the nation's most important public challenges. CX provides technical assistance and publications to individuals and organizations working toward that end. For free assistance, contact CX, 1120 G Street N.W., Suite 730, Washington, D.C. 20005; phone: (202) 393-1441; fax: (202) 626-4978; e-mail: congex@congex.org.

References

Aicher, P. J. "The Study Circle Experience in Sweden Compared with the United States." *Option: Journal of the Folk Education Association of America,* Fall 1991, *15* (2), 17–23.

Arvidson, L. "The Study Circle Library in a Historical Perspective." Paper presented at International Association of Learning for Adults Conference, Stockholm, 1990.

Ashby, N. L. "Talking About Racism." *Humanities,* Sept.-Oct. 1997, *18* (5), 33.

Bainter, R., Lhevine, P., Okubo, D., Leighninger, M., and McGrath, M. "Four Communities on the Cutting Edge of Change: Seattle, Washington; Lee's Summit, Missouri; Lima, Ohio; and Bronx County, New York." *National Civic Review,* Fall 1998, *87* (3), 201–212.

Burch, G. (ed.). *Accent on Learning: An Analytical History of the Fund for Adult Education's Experimental Discussion Project, 1951–1959.* Pasadena, Calif.: Fund for Adult Education, 1960.

Edelson, P. J. "Socrates on the Assembly Line: The Ford Foundation's Mass Marketing of Liberal Adult Education." Paper presented at the annual conference of the Midwest History of Education Society, Chicago, Oct. 1991.

Flavin-McDonald, C., with Higgins, D., Necci Dineen, J., McCoy, M., and Sokolowski, R. "New Castle County, Delaware: Study Circles on Racism and Race Relations, Year 1— 1997, A Report on the Focus Groups." Study Circles Resource Center and the YWCA of New Castle County, 1998.

Gould, J. E. *The Chautauqua Movement: An Episode in the Continuing American Revolution.* New York: State University of New York, 1961.

Kurland, N. D. "The Scandinavian Study Circle: An Idea for the United States." *The College Board Review,* Winter 1979–80, *114.* Reprinted in *Lifelong Learning: The Adult Years,* Feb. 1982, pp. 24–30.

Leighninger, M. "Study Circles on Race Connect Talk with Action: Many Voices Are Answering Clinton's Call." *Focus on Study Circles,* Fall 1997, pp. 3, 8.

Mattson, K. *Creating a Democratic Public: The Struggle for Urban Participatory Democracy During the Progressive Era.* University Park: The Pennsylvania State University Press, 1998.

McCoy, M. "Engaging the Public in Discussions of Race." In P. Reichler and P. B. Dredge (eds.), *Governing Diverse Communities: A Focus on Race and Ethnic Relations.* Washington, D.C.: National League of Cities, 1997.

Oliver, L. P. *Study Circles: Coming Together for Personal Growth and Social Change.* Washington, D.C./Cabin John, Md.: Seven Locks Press, 1987.

Oliver, L. P. "Study Circles: Individual Growth Through Collaborative Learning." In L. Cavaliere and A. Sgroi (eds.), *Learning for Personal Development.* New Directions for Adult and Continuing Education, no. 53. San Francisco: Jossey-Bass, 1992.

Putnam, R. D. "Bowling Alone: America's Declining Social Capital." *Journal of Democracy,* Jan. 1995, pp. 85–97.

Wuthnow, R. *Sharing the Journey: Support Groups and America's New Quest for Community.* New York: Free Press, 1994.

CATHERINE FLAVIN-MCDONALD *is program director, material development and research, at the Study Circles Resource Center.*

MOLLY HOLME BARRETT *is project coordinator and assistant editor at the Study Circles Resource Center.*

The philosophy behind the creativity centers in The Netherlands has been shifting between a focus on the intrinsic values of art itself and the instrumental use of art for developmental and social purposes.

The Dutch Experiment in Developing Adult Creativity

Folkert H. Haanstra

In The Netherlands, there are two main institutions outside the schools for education in the arts: music schools and creativity centers. The first music schools were founded in the nineteenth century as loosely formed organizations of private music teachers. Institutions that today offer courses in drawing and crafts with utilitarian industrial goals also originated in the nineteenth century (Asselbergs-Neessen and Van der Kamp, 1992). In contrast, the first so-called creativity center was founded in Amsterdam in 1947 by a group of progressive artists and teachers who did not approve of the art education in schools at the time. The number of creativity centers rose in the following decades to about one hundred. In addition to the visual arts (painting, graphics, sculpture, ceramics, textile art), these centers offer courses in drama, dance, and photography. Although the first centers were intended as both an innovation and a complement to art education for schoolchildren, adults have gradually come to make up the majority of students. At present, there are 262 art education centers: 150 music schools, 66 creativity centers, and 46 combined centers for the arts. Yearly, about 390,000 students (almost 3 percent of the Dutch population) take courses at these centers.

This chapter describes how the centers have developed and diverged along two major models, and it addresses the question of the extent to which the different goals of art education have been demonstrated.

Creativity Centers: The First Decades

The notion of art education for creative development and "free expression" dominated the philosophy of the creativity centers during the 1960s and 1970s. The Association of Creativity Centers formulated the main goal of the centers as "the development of creative abilities by means derived from the arts" (VCO, 1979). Experiencing the process of creation was considered more important than the final product. The assumption was that art can play an important role in developing the creative potential and that art through self-expression can develop the self. Self-expression was defined as giving vent in constructive forms to one's feelings, emotions, and thoughts at one's own level of development.

Working with children was part of the artistic liberation of the artists involved in the first creativity centers. These were the years when abstract expressionism became mainstream in the art world. In the 1960s, the gap between art education and the professional arts gradually widened. The new theories in art and their visualizations in such forms as pop art, minimal art, and conceptual art had little in common with the activities and work of the adult students at the creativity centers, who were wrestling with the more traditional problems of representation, expression, and form.

The widening gap between developments in art education at the centers and developments in the professional arts can also be illustrated by the way in which the VCO described the difference between amateur art and art education. According to a VCO policy paper (1979), in amateur art the end product is the first matter of importance, and the established professional arts are followed as an example. In art education, the professional arts do not serve as a norm for quality. In art education, the personal meanings derived from the arts are used in educational processes, and these meanings may serve many different social and emotional purposes. It should be added that, in contrast to the creativity centers, music schools had a more discipline-based, art-intrinsic orientation, and as a consequence had (and still have) closer ties with amateur musicians.

In the late 1970s and early 1980s, some art educators and policymakers began to sound a note of warning against the prevailing instrumental goals of the creativity centers and the gap that was seen to exist between professional art and education in the arts. Kassies (1981) expressed his concern about the shifting reasoning behind art education. He stated that beauty and cultural heritage, creativity and self-actualization, political awareness and emancipation, and most recently, leisure, have been used to justify art and art education. Emphasis on these instrumental goals resulted in an underestimation of the "autonomous force of the practice of art" (Kassies, 1981, p. 4). He hoped for a reassessment of this autonomous function. At the opening of a new creativity center, the Dutch minister of welfare, health, and culture supported Kassies's view. "To consider art education as an instrument for changing society or a means toward self-actualization has in most instances proven to be a plea for eating soup with a fork" (Brinkman, 1983, p. 3). According to the minister, art education had to accept that it is not its task to meet all kinds of needs, interests, and desires of people, however genuine they may be. Learning in the arts can only indirectly contribute to the sensory, intellectual, and emotional development of individuals. As in the years of the first creativity center, art education should once again develop in direct interaction with the arts and be inspired by professional artists.

This call for a return to intrinsic goals was strengthened by external pressures on art education outside schools. Creativity centers form part of a city or region's social-cultural facilities. Although most creativity centers are private foundations, about 70 percent of their budget is provided by local subsidies and 30 percent by course fees. In the face of the severe financial problems that beset many cities during the 1980s, the role of the creativity centers came under increasingly close scrutiny as municipalities sought to balance their budgets. More than ever the centers needed to provide a convincing justification for their existence compared with other social and cultural facilities, such as youth clubs and centers for the elderly. In this competition, emphasizing social goals of art activities that other organizations also stressed seemed less fruitful than emphasizing the unique character of the centers, which is rooted in the arts. Unlike the other institutions, which used the arts as only one means for social participation, the centers were committed to the arts as an autonomous domain. They could offer a place both for passing on a cultural heritage and for renewing culture.

Two Models: Intrinsic Versus Instrumental Goals

In the mid-1980s, case studies were carried out in two creativity centers with opposing views on art education. The first was the center in the city of Den Bosch, which emphasized cultural pluralism and the instrumental and developmental uses of art; the second was the center in the city of Tilburg, which emphasized the intrinsic values of art and the close ties between art education and the professional arts (Haanstra, 1986). It was hypothesized that these different justifications would shape the practical functioning of the centers at all levels: the kind of external relationships they maintain with professional art institutions, their recruitment of teachers and enrollment of participants, the content and degree of prescriptiveness of their curricula, and so on.

Comparison of the cases confirmed some of the projected discrepancies. The Tilburg center, which adhered to art-intrinsic goals, rejected the recruitment of special target groups. "We have something to offer that we think is important and interesting to all kinds of people. The fact that you are unemployed or that you are a woman is of no importance in our view of art education," the director stated. In contrast, the Den Bosch center aimed at special target groups for whom, it was believed, art was a vehicle for personal development and emancipation. Special courses were organized for the unemployed, women, the elderly, and the mentally handicapped. The center also offered courses with open registration. Their content was generally comparable to those at Tilburg, except that at Den Bosch some courses on what may be called the popular arts were also offered, such as folk dancing, puppet making, floral decoration, and special kinds of needlework. These courses were not on the program at Tilburg because they were not considered to originate from official art disciplines.

At Tilburg, being a professional artist was a prerequisite for teaching, and when filling a vacancy the applicants' artistic achievements would be judged first. Teachers considered their own professional art activities as an essential factor in their courses. Characteristically, the common term *artist-teacher* was avoided; one spoke merely of *artists*. Most of the teachers considered their own professional art activities as the essential factor in their lessons. In contrast, at Den Bosch having a professional career as an artist was not a requirement. Instead, emphasis was placed on didactic skills and the ability to handle a group.

It was expected that the Tilburg center, which was striving for art-intrinsic goals, would use curricula with a considerable degree of prescriptiveness. To ascertain that the desired knowledge and skills would be acquired, the aims, content, and sequence the teacher uses should be defined in advance. In contrast, a center that bases its activities on a more subjective justification was expected to use open-ended curricula, because the personal needs of participants should determine aims and content. However, in both centers a high degree of prescriptiveness of curricula was in fact rejected. Reasons for this rejection are partly historical, because the rule-governed curricula stand for an educational system the centers were firmly opposed to in the past. Other reasons are that the participants form a heterogeneous group requiring individual supervision and that the very nature of art education contradicts prescribed outcomes. Most of the artist-teachers use what Eisner (1979) calls *problem-solving objectives*. This means the artist poses a problem (for example, the creation of an art product) for which different solutions are possible, but these solutions have to meet a set of criteria or specifications. In advanced courses *expressive activities* (to use Eisner's terminology again) dominate. This means that participants explore or focus on issues they consider of interest or importance to themselves and to the artist-teacher.

Creativity Centers in the 1990s

During the late 1980s and the early 1990s the more intrinsic art-oriented goals gradually gained strength. A telling detail is that many centers are no longer called creativity centers at all, but rather *centers for education in the arts*. The director of the Association of Centers for Art Education (VKV) formulates the general goal as "to contribute directly to both the productive and the receptive cultural participation of the population, which means to contribute to practicing different art disciplines and to becoming receptive to the art of others" (Van Muilekom, 1994, p. 9). No longer are the courses exclusively productive. Courses in art history and art criticism have become a part of the programs. A number of centers have started to offer preparatory courses for art academies.

In addition to the renewed relationship with professional art, a more open relationship with amateur art is meaningful as well. Both aspects will be described in the following sections.

Beyond Creating. About 80 percent of the centers offer activities such as visits to museums and theaters, and most centers plan to expand this kind of educational activity (B&A Groep, 1995). About 70 percent offer courses in art analysis or art theory. In addition to these separate activities and courses, centers strive for courses in which art making, art analysis, and visits to professional art productions are integrated. A study by Verhulst, Völker, and Driessen (1995) concludes that in this respect the outcomes are somewhat disappointing. Only about 10 percent of the teachers regularly combine art making with visits to museums, theaters, or cinemas. More than half of the teachers never do this, and few teachers bring relevant plays, exhibitions, or concerts to the attention of the participants in their courses.

Case studies of two creativity centers that developed new activities showed gains and losses (Kooyman and Verhagen, 1991). Courses and workshops that explicitly included art analysis attracted new audiences, but not all of the regular participants were willing to accept the new content. As one of the teachers said, "Most of these people come to learn to paint and not to learn to analyze art. In their view, the time devoted to art analysis and art history is more or less a waste of time." This finding is in line with several studies into the motivations of participants of arts centers (for example, Stevens, 1989; Verhulst, Völker, and Driessen, 1995; Haanstra, 1998). These motives concern first of all learning artistic skills and techniques. Most participants find pleasure in being able to make an etching, dance in a certain style, or play an instrument. In general, participants are satisfied with the courses the centers offer, especially insofar as they meet their wish for learning skills and techniques.

Second come social motives, such as meeting with people who share the same interests, being in good company, sharing a meaningful hobby, and so on. Only a few participants state that a better understanding of the professional art world is one of their motives.

Relationship with Amateur Art. As mentioned earlier, the Association of Creativity Centers used to emphasize the differences between amateur art and art education as product-oriented versus process-oriented. Striving for qualitative products has now become quite acceptable in the centers. Some also have a service function—for instance, offering a sound studio, theater facilities, or exhibition space to amateur artists. Results of a nationwide questionnaire (Verhulst, Völker, and Driessen, 1995) show that 58 percent of the art centers yearly have some kind of collaboration with a club or association of amateurs; most of these collaborations are music projects.

There is a structural cooperation between many music schools and brass bands, and many amateur choirs make use of the music school facilities. In the other disciplines, such as visual arts and theater, such cooperation often depends on initiatives of individual teachers. Even though the "market" of amateur artists is a promising one for arts centers that has not been developed systematically, some needs assessments among amateurs show the limits of this market. Only a part of the amateur audience needs education, coaching, or some other support by art centers. Many of these individuals are not members of official organizations of amateurs. Beckers (1990) points out that for amateurs, autonomy and self-sufficiency are essential. Moreover, in the visual arts the amateurs who actually are members of amateur organizations tend to have a traditional view of art, with a strong preference for premodernist realistic landscapes, still lifes, and portraits. Many artist-teachers who consider visual art more than mimetic representations find it difficult to adapt to the needs of these amateurs.

Present Dilemmas

In the last decade, art centers have been confronted with conflicting demands. First of all, they are expected to offer courses that meet high qualitative standards of both content and method and to keep fruitful relationships with both the professional and the amateur art worlds. Second, they are expected to reach all levels of the population. For decades, the Dutch national government and local authorities have been trying to stimulate cultural participation in all groups and levels of the population. For local authorities, the representation of all levels of the population among art center students is an important issue, one obvious reason for this being that these centers are relatively expensive. Participants at the art centers come from different income groups, but levels of education are not equally represented. Several studies indicate substantial overrepresentation of the higher educated among the participants at creativity centers and music schools (Kooyman and Verhagen, 1991; Verhulst, Völker, and Driessen, 1995; Haanstra, 1998). Although there are no exact figures, art centers assume that immigrants are underrepresented as well.

Centers have looked for solutions in different areas. One solution is to accept the unequal representation of the population and increase course fees. This limits the dependence on the local government but of course strengthens the selective participation in the population. Other strategies are based on attracting a broader audience. Although the centers have been reluctant to use commercial strategies like marketing, many now have started to use marketing instruments. This implies a more client-centered approach and a wider acceptance of adapting the courses to the preferences of special target groups. With or without marketing, some centers have already introduced courses that do not derive their content solely from the classical autonomous arts but are related to the popular arts and youth culture.

Offering activities for special target groups often implies that besides artistic production (as in the Tilburg model) other goals are strived for (as in the Den Bosch model). The conflict between the two models has not been overcome, and the debate over the philosophy behind the centers continues.

Empirical Research into the Effects of Art Education

The question that urges itself on those debating the justification of art centers, and of art education in general, is to what extent the wide range of goals can be substantiated by empirical proof. A study by Haanstra (1994) describes several reviews of intervention studies in art education. The majority of the outcome research deals with primary and secondary education. About 15 percent deals with nonschool settings, such as museums, creativity centers, and community programs for the elderly. Most research is carried out in music education and in the visual arts. Although there is a growing body of research into drama and dance education, controlled evaluations of drama and especially of dance are scarce. In most cases, the learning effects of a short program or a small number of lessons are studied. Few studies are aimed at curricula that last one or more semesters. Furthermore, effects are mostly measured directly or within a short period after finishing the program.

On the basis of the collected studies, four categories of instrumental learning effects of art education were determined, as were four categories of intrinsic effects.

Instrumental Effects. The four categories of instrumental learning effects are these: *cognition* (mental abilities such as verbal and arithmetical abilities, visual-spatial abilities, memory, attention span, creative thinking, and problem solving); *perceptual motor skills* (eye-hand coordination, body control, color discrimination, pitch and loudness discrimination); *personality, attitude, and social behavior* (self-concept, self-esteem, emotional well-being, social behavior such as social adjustment, and non-art-related attitudes and values such as academic motivation or racial prejudice); and *academic achievement* (improvement in reading or mathematics).

Intrinsic Effects. The four main categories of intrinsic learning effects of art education are these: *art production skills* (for example, musical performance or, in the visual arts, the handling of different materials and techniques, pictorial depth representation, or the expressive and creative quality of art products); *knowledge and understanding* (facts and figures of art history, music history, the art vocabulary that is being used in art criticism); *attitudes and values* (interest in art and participation in cultural activities); and *aesthetic perception* (the informed perception of art objects).

A wide range of intrinsic effects of art education has been demonstrated. They involve short-term effects on knowledge and skills but also long-term effects, like practicing art as a hobby in later life, visiting museums, going to concerts, and the like. From Dutch cultural statistics it is known that participants at art centers *do* visit more museums and go to more concerts, theater, or dance performances than the average citizen. Research shows that the relationship is in part an immediate effect of the courses taken at the centers (Nagel and Ganzeboom, 1996). However, it is also true that people who come from culturally active families and who are more culturally active in their youth are more likely to participate in amateur art and art centers in later life.

Research findings concerning instrumental effects often are contradictory and unconvincing. Two closely related reasons for this general outcome have been put forward. In the first place, bringing about instrumental effects in general presupposes a larger amount of transfer of learning than does bringing about intrinsic, domain-specific effects. Second, in research, measurement problems tend to increase as the amount of transfer is increased.

Conclusion

The philosophical pendulum justifying the art centers has been swinging between utility and uniqueness, between art as a means and art as a goal in itself. It is not always easy to draw the line between the rhetoric of art advocacy and what the artist-teachers in the centers thought to be realistic and attainable goals in relation to the arts. Besides a sizable amount of opportunism there has been a firm and sincere belief in what art education is capable of in terms of larger impact on people's lives.

In formulating their goals, the first centers presupposed a general transfer of creative skills, traits, and attitudes employed in the arts to nonartistic tasks and situations. The implicit assumption was that transfer takes care of itself. But research shows that the centers' far-reaching claims of profound psychological change toward a creative personality were naive. In those days, many held the view that the arts belonged to the affective domain and were mainly appreciated as an antidote to cognitive-oriented education. But the view that the arts themselves are cognitive activities has become more widely accepted. In this perspective, different forms of intelligence are discerned, linked to particular symbol systems such as language, logic, and mathematics but also to the musical symbol system, the visual-spatial, and the bodily kinesthetic. These different modes of thinking make unique forms of meaning possible, and individuals have the potential to develop competence in each of these intelligences (Gardner, 1993). There is no separate artistic intelligence, but each of the forms of intelligence can be directed toward aesthetic as well as nonaesthetic ends. The centrality of spatial thinking in the visual arts is self-evident, and dance can be described as one of the domains in which the bodily kinesthetic intelligence can express itself. Basically, this is an intrinsic, domain-specific view on the worth of art education, but Gardner does not rule out the possibility of the transfer of art learning. Artistic activities can be seen as occasions for mental activity, some shared with other pursuits, others special moments in the arts. This implies the possibility that cognitive dispositions developed in the different art forms can be applied to nonartistic domains. This view on the potential of art education for general cognitive abilities has been adopted and put into practice by art teachers in secondary education in The Netherlands. It emphasizes problem-solving processes in the arts.

This cognitive orientation has not yet received much support in the art centers. Until recently, the centers have focused their attention more and more on high-quality art production and more passive activities, such as guided visits to museums and concerts. But centers are now beginning to realize that in the long run this policy will be too limited. Eventually, it will lead to an even more selective audience and there will be no difference between the art centers and private organizations offering art activities.

If the centers want continued support from their municipalities, a broader function for the general public is called for. A more cognitive approach toward art education for adults is one of the views that can guide innovation in the centers. The centers now face the difficult task of relating the ideals of the post-war years with current insights into the possibilities of art education.

References

Asselbergs-Neessen, V., and Van der Kamp, M. *Van Snieschoule tot centrum voor kunstzinnige vorming. Honderd jaar School voor Handenarbeid 1892–1992.* Groningen: Van Dijk & Voorthuis Regio-Project, 1992.

B&A Groep. *Het LOKV op weg.* Utrecht: LOKV, 1995.

Beckers, T. "De oprechte amateur: pleidooi voor de ware liefhebber." *Kunsten & Educatie,* 1990, *3* (1), 13–19.

Brinkman, E. "Soep met een vork." *VCO-Bulletin,* 1983, *28,* 2–3.

Eisner, E. *The Educational Imagination: On the Design and Evaluation of School Programs.* Old Tappan, N.J.: Macmillan, 1979.

Gardner, H. *Multiple Intelligences: The Theory in Practice.* New York: Basic Books, 1993.

Haanstra, F. "Creativity Centers in the Netherlands: Policy and Practice." *Journal of Art & Design Education,* 1986, *5* (1, 2), 81–90.

Haanstra, F. *Effects of Art Education on Visual-Spatial Ability and Aesthetic Perception: Two Meta-Analyses.* Amsterdam: Thesis, 1994.

Haanstra, F. *Buitenschoolse Kunsteducatie in Dordrecht.* Amsterdam: SCO-Kohnstamm Instituut, 1998.

Kassies, J. "Toespraak bij het afscheid van Jan van Oosten." *VCO-Bulletin,* 1981, *20,* 2–4.

Kooyman, R., and Verhagen, K. *Kunsteducatie & participanten: profielen van docenten en deelnemers in de kunsteducatie.* Utrecht: LOKV, 1991.

Nagel, I., and Ganzeboom, H. *Cultuurdeelname in de levensloop.* Utrecht: LOKV, 1996.

Stevens, G. T. *Het rendement van kunstzinnige vorming.* Nijmegen: Dienst Sociale Zaken Gemeente Nijmegen, 1989.

Van Muilekom, J. *Kunstzinnige vorming: een onderneming. Continuïteit en vernieuwing in de kunstzinnige vorming.* Utrecht: VKV, 1994.

VCO. *Het beleid van de VCO: Naar een samenhang in de kunstzinnige vorming.* Amsterdam: Vereniging voor Creativiteitsontwikkeling, 1979.

Verhulst, C.T.A.M., Völker, B. G., and Driessen, F. *Samenwerking tussen kunsteducatie, amateurkunst en professionele kunst: Verslag van een onderzoek.* Utrecht: LOKV, 1995.

FOLKERT H. HAANSTRA is senior researcher at the SCO-Kohnstamm Institute for Educational Research of the University of Amsterdam.

A professional development program can be an exercise in creative design and delivery when ideas come from multiple sources and the program itself is continually being reinvented.

The Harvard Management for Lifelong Education Program: Creative Approaches to Designing a Professional Development Program

Clifford Baden

The Harvard Institute for the Management of Lifelong Education (MLE) is a professional development program for leaders in postsecondary lifelong education programs. This annual two-week residential program was first offered in the summer of 1979. Since its inception, it has been cosponsored by the Harvard Graduate School of Education and the Office of Adult Learning Services at the College Board. Cliff Baden, who has written this article in a self-interview format, has served as director of the program since 1984.

Program Founding and Development

To begin, can you tell us something about the program you found when you arrived in 1984?

The story should start even earlier, with the founding of the MLE program. In 1978, Fred Jacobs, who was the director of Programs in Professional Education at Harvard, and Rex Moon, who was the head of a new venture at the College Board called Future Directions for a Learning Society, were brought together by Frank Keppel. Frank was a distinguished member of the faculty at the Harvard Graduate School of Education. All three of these people recognized that the face of higher education was changing as increasing numbers of adults were pursuing lifelong education. Some of this was happening, of course, in informal settings or in community-based adult education programs. But much of it was happening on the college and university campuses of this country. And this phenomenon raised a lot of interesting questions for faculty members and administrators. Who were these adult learners, and why were they appearing on campus? What kinds of courses or programs were they looking for? What would be the implications for teaching and curriculum? What kinds of support services would institutions have to provide? How should an institution market programs for lifelong learners? How should it finance them? How should it evaluate these programs? Questions such as these deserved serious attention.

Ten years earlier, Harvard had created a professional development program that convened senior leadership in colleges and universities. Based on the success of that program—the Institute for Educational Management—the Harvard Graduate School of Education made plans to launch a new professional development program to serve faculty and administrators of lifelong education programs, primarily in higher education settings. The planners received start-up funding from the Sears-Roebuck Foundation. They established a national advisory board. Their design called for a two-week residential program for about seventy-five people to be held in Cambridge, Massachusetts, once a year in the summer.

Now, twenty years later, when the program is so well established, it's hard to appreciate what a leap of faith this was. The originators had enough foresight to understand that lifelong education was a significant factor in American higher education and would continue to play an important role. They believed they could bring practitioners together and convene conversations that were deeper and more provocative than those you might find at a typical conference. And while I don't know if they ever articulated it quite this way, I think that by offering such a program at a university like Harvard they were somehow dignifying the important work of people in continuing education and extension programs—they were saying to the broader community, "This is a subject that is worthy of serious attention."

And when you arrived in 1984 . . . ?

When I arrived in the spring of 1984, I met my new colleague, Bob Kegan, a faculty member at the Harvard Graduate School of Education and a distinguished scholar in the area of adult development. Bob had just been invited to serve as educational chair of the MLE program. Together, we decided that we would observe the summer 1984 session of MLE, which had been planned many months before by our predecessors, and then, after the summer, we would decide what changes if any we wanted to introduce into the program.

What we found in 1984 was a solid program that was attracting the right audience. Most of the faculty for the program came from Harvard, but the faculty also included some distinguished practitioners, such as Morris Keeton, the former president of Antioch and the founder of CAEL, and Hal Miller, the dean of continuing education at the University of Minnesota. The program structure was essentially a succession of presentations on a dozen different topics.

Bob Kegan and I wanted to build on the original foundation, but we also wanted to shape something substantially different. First and foremost, we decided to place a high value on the quality of teaching in the program. We would invite to teach in the program only those people who were outstanding teachers, who could engage the participants actively in stimulating conversations.

We were also concerned about what the total learning experience of this two-week program would be for the participants. That's a consideration that is too often ignored in program design. Program planners will often focus on "filling the slots" in the schedule with good speakers on preselected topics. We wanted to move the learners to the center of our thinking as we attended to the usual questions of who would be teaching what topics, in what formats, and in what sequence. And we also thought about the rhythm of the days and of the weeks. What would happen in class, and out of class? What would be the balance of classtime, and studying, and small-group work, and social activities? How was the learner going to experience this program?

We also made one important decision, which was to give ourselves the luxury of knowing that we did not have to get the program perfect the first time. Of course, we tried to make it as good as we could from the very first redesign. But we also expected that the program would continue for several years into the future, and we would have multiple opportunities to observe, to rethink, to tinker, to adjust it as we went along. That important insight—that we were creating a work in progress—was ultimately very liberating.

Program Redesign

You talk about the program that "we" delivered. I take it that you and Bob Kegan worked on the redesign together?

Yes, and we've continued to work closely together on the program in all the years since then. I can't emphasize enough the importance of a good partner in the creative process, especially one who complements your own skills. Bob, who is a developmental psychologist, has wonderful insights into ways to make people comfortable—psychologically—in the learning community we're trying to create at MLE. He puts both the participants and the faculty at ease. He sets a tone that he calls "playfully serious and seriously playful." He encourages the participants to open themselves to new experiences, knowing that they are in a safe space.

My own strengths are in designing an administrative infrastructure that allows people to learn. I attend to such issues as identifying excellent support staff, thinking through all the logistical elements that play an important role in the program, identifying new faculty and new topics for the program, developing new curriculum materials, and so on.

Each of us depends on the other for insights, for suggestions, for support. You've certainly read in the literature about the benefits of putting together a team whose members bring different strengths and interests, because you'll get a better product than any one person could deliver alone. In this instance, that has certainly proved to be true.

You make it sound very easy. Did you run into any snags along the way?

It's important to stay alert to potential barriers to creative program development. Probably the most pernicious of these are the doubters or the naysayers in your organization, who tell you "We've always done it this way." Sometimes that gets voiced as, "Are you sure that will work?" Well, no, we're not always sure something will work, but we're willing to experiment to find out if it does; we're willing to learn from our mistakes. We've certainly had our share of less-than-perfect moments over the years—faculty members who didn't connect well with the group, overambitious scheduling, the inevitable logistical snafus. But our audiences—the participants in the program—have almost always been tolerant of those mistakes, because they get so many other signals that we are trying to put together a program that is in their best interest.

Your original program redesign was in 1985. What's happened to the program since then?

To stick with your theme of creativity, I'd say that our greatest creativity has come in the years since then, in the continuous process of program renewal and updating. The program in 1998 would be virtually unrecognizable to someone who had attended in 1985. All the case studies that we use are new; two-thirds of the faculty are new over that same period. And no, we have never had a master plan for how this would evolve; we've created it by doing it, from year to year.

Without going into detail on the program content or structure, can you suggest some of the more "macro" ways in which the program has changed?

Sure. First, we intentionally broadened the audience for MLE. In the first years of the program, for example, there were virtually no participants from community colleges. And yet those schools are doing some of the most interesting, creative work in higher education, and they serve an extraordinarily diverse group of students—truly lifelong learners. So now about 30 percent of each MLE class consists of leaders from community colleges.

The next thing we did, over several years, was refocus the curriculum on topics that were salient no matter what kind of institution participants came from: topics like leadership, and strategy, and organizational change.

Most recently, I'd say we've been trying to keep up with the changes in higher education generally and reflect those in our curriculum and in the participants we accept into the program. It was always true that the people who were coming to MLE and profiting the most from their experience were the people who were responsible for making interesting changes happen on their campuses. They were the ones who were serving new groups of learners, in new ways, with new programs, in new locations, using new technologies. They were the people who were creating and managing interinstitutional alliances. They were the ones who were creating partnerships with business and industry and the community. They had many different titles, but what they had in common was the responsibility for leading innovation and change. So that theme—leading innovation and change—became more prominent in the MLE program over the years. Our challenge has been to identify interesting change scenarios and leadership challenges that are both up-to-date and useful for teaching purposes.

Second, we've seen that on most campuses today our original concept of lifelong education—that is, the practice of innovation and entrepreneurship and new program development on behalf of learners—is no longer relegated to a single unit like continuing education or extension. There are many, many people on campuses nowadays who are responsible for serving new learners in new ways. These are people sitting in central administration, in positions of significant authority. So the challenge to us, to our creativity, has been to find ways to open up the program to a much broader audience of educational leaders, all of whom are responsible for leading their institutions in new directions.

Getting New Ideas

Where do you get the ideas that result in the changes to the program from year to year?

One important source of ideas and inspiration and support comes from our national advisory board. That's a ten-person board that meets once a year, after the program, to discuss what has gone well and what could be improved. They get into good substantive discussions of changes in higher education. The annual board meetings are like a private seminar for the MLE program staff. Board members also keep us current on what's happening in the field, through phone calls, e-mail messages, and their publications.

Where else do you get ideas?

Some of the obvious places, like the annual conferences of professional associations, just to see what's being talked about—and to make sure that the MLE program doesn't replicate what people might hear at a traditional conference. We want to be aware of what the current issues are, but we try to find ways to talk about them that can bring new and deeper insights.

Another source of ideas is the press, such as the *Chronicle of Higher Education*. I read the papers faithfully to make sure that I'm up-to-date on what's happening. I typically cut out at least one article a week, and I put it in my "idea" file for next year's MLE program. It might be an idea for a new faculty member, or a new topic we may want to introduce into the curriculum, or an idea for a way to update an existing segment of the curriculum, or a book or a report that I'll want look at to see if there's some way we might use it in the program. Only a few of these ideas will actually make it into the following year's program, but they represent a way for me to keep my own creative juices flowing throughout the year.

Can you say anything about the role of the faculty who teach in the program?

That's a very important point. We've been blessed with a core group of faculty who have been with the program for many years. They enjoy teaching at MLE, and the participants respond very well to their teaching. What makes them such valuable colleagues is their openness to new ideas. They are very willing to try out new curricular materials, especially to incorporate new case studies from the field. They've allowed us to play with innovative teaching schedules, and in several instances they've suggested those themselves. Perhaps the most fun for me has been finding ways for them to work together, to coteach sessions that allow participants to analyze the same material from different perspectives.

Each year we will typically have at least one person teaching at MLE who is new to the program. That does several things for us. First and most obviously, it's a way to ensure that we're getting new voices and new topics into the curriculum. But it also keeps the staff and especially the other faculty on their toes, listening to what the new person is saying and how she or he is saying it, and then trying to find ways to build on this new material in other sessions throughout the program.

Do you get any insights from the participants in the program?

Absolutely! Feedback from our participants is one of the most important sources of continuing creativity for us. While the program is in session each year, we're talking to them all the time and listening very hard as they tell stories about what's happening on their campuses. A relatively recent innovation for us is that we ask each participant to write a brief case study about a leadership dilemma at his or her institution. Those minicase studies get used in the MLE curriculum, but they are also a very important source of insight for us into the kinds of issues our participants are dealing with on a day-to-day basis. And finally, we take the program evaluation process very seriously. We learn a great deal from the evaluations about what's working well and what is not. We generate a list each year of the things we will do differently next time around.

I should say, too, that our participants have been ahead of us in one important way. Over the past three or four years, a broader spectrum of leadership in higher education has looked at the MLE program and realized it was right for them and for what was going on in their institutions. And so MLE has found itself enrolling more and more vice presidents and provosts and department and division heads. We've fine-tuned our curriculum in response to this more eclectic audience. We've also adapted our marketing significantly to reflect what the market was telling us about our own program—that it was attractive and relevant to a broad leadership audience in higher education.

The MLE Program and Creativity

MLE is essentially a leadership program, and some would argue that creativity is an important element in leadership. Does the MLE program teach creativity?

We don't teach creativity per se; rather, we try to provide a space in which creative and innovative ideas can flourish. Let me give you two examples. The first is to be found in the way we structure the MLE curriculum. Traditional curriculum design presents a speaker on a topic, then that speaker disappears, and a new speaker arrives, and so on. In the design of MLE, each faculty member works with the group over several days, at oddly spaced intervals. This introduces variety into each day. Also, as I mentioned before, it makes it easier for faculty to sit in on one another's sessions and build on the insights that come out of one another's classes. But I think, too, that this kind of nonlinear, discontinuous processing of material by participants can lead to unexpected insights, to unanticipated connections.

A second design element that fosters creativity is our use of small discussion groups that meet every day. Now, there is nothing original in the use of small groups. What may be different is that we form these groups so that they are as heterogeneous as we can possibly make them, along every possible dimension. And then each group has a great deal of flexibility in regard to where it will meet, when it will meet, and even what it will choose to focus on as a group. Some groups will decide to use their time together to review what went on in the large plenary sessions. Others will want to spend time together discussing the assignments for the next day. And increasingly, groups are devoting their time to discussion of leadership dilemmas that the group members are facing on their own campuses. The groups are a safe space in which to apply the collective wisdom of the participants and the insights from the formal MLE curriculum to the real-life issues facing individual leaders. And participants have told us that useful, creative solutions do result from this process of brainstorming in discussion groups.

The way the discussion groups function at MLE is a direct reflection of the feedback we have received from participants in the program over the years. The role of the discussion groups has evolved from something much more structured to what we have today. And I expect that, like so many other aspects of the program, this too will continue to evolve. Although we retain many of the strongest elements of the program design from one year to the next, in fact the program is in a constant state of reinvention.

Certainly all of us who work on MLE have a set of core commitments: to high-quality teaching, to good practice of adult education principles, to creating a learning space that is psychologically and physically comfortable, to stimulating both personal and professional growth in educational leaders. And these commitments don't change. But what I most enjoy about the program is finding new ways to express those core commitments, by incorporating new information from the field of practice, by constantly revisiting the curriculum, the faculty, the schedule, the logistics, and so on.

In summary, what are key lessons about creativity in program design that you might share with others, based on the MLE experience?

Let me qualify my response by saying that it is based on my experience in developing a program that is offered not just once, but rather on a recurring basis.

1. *Find good partners*—people who care about the same things you do but who bring complementary interests and strengths. Creativity is often risky and lonely, and it's good to know you're not trying to do it all alone. Having people with whom you can bounce ideas back and forth is likely to lead to a better program than if you tried to do it all alone.
2. *Get good ideas and good data from multiple sources.* Many programs establish advisory committees. Too often, though, those committees exist primarily to lend credibility to the program, or they help with marketing the program. Those functions are important, but as the manager or designer of a program, what you most need are reliable sources of good ideas. You won't be able to implement every idea you hear, but the process of hearing them and filtering them can lead to a better final program. Put systems in place for yourself for generating creative ideas.
3. *Recruit outsiders*—to "sit in" on your program, to participate in it as new faculty, or simply to observe, as board members or as trusted colleagues from a different discipline. Outsiders will see things you don't see and hear things that you don't hear. Debrief them. They can be an excellent source of new insights and ideas.
4. *When the program is not in session, find multiple ways to get new ideas.* Network. Talk to graduates of the program. Go to conferences and meetings and keep your antennae up. Read journal articles and newspaper articles. Keep a file of clippings and ideas. Read the literature in allied disciplines, looking for new angles on your own work.
5. *Look upon your program as a work in progress.* Any given iteration will be the best you know how to make it at that point. But the next session represents an opportunity to make it even better.
6. *If you are the director of the program, then your role is to be the glue that holds all these ideas together*—all this creativity, all this energy. As John Kao wrote in his book *Jamming,* your role is to "define the overall 'sound' of the enterprise, generate a terrific environment, establish standards of quality, bring in great people, provision creative efforts with needed resources, and establish boundary conditions such as budgets and schedules" (1997, p. 99).

And while I have Kao's book in hand, here's another passage that captures much of what is happening when things are going well in a program like MLE. Someone might observe the program, he writes, "and think: *These people are having too much fun.* Don't be fooled. All those people are working very hard. But they're having a great time because their creative juices are flowing, and their work has meaning. That charged and playful atmosphere doesn't simply materialize. Savvy managers, who send a constant, consistent message that they value creativity, work assiduously to devise an environment that ignites everyone's enthusiasm. Creativity becomes a process, not an event" (p. 79).

Designing and delivering programs that can help professionals grow is tremendously satisfying work. The fact that it is a creative, constantly self-renewing process also makes it a great deal of fun.

Reference

Kao, J. *Jamming: The Art and Discipline of Business Creativity.* New York: HarperCollins, 1997.

CLIFFORD BADEN *is the director of Programs in Professional Education at the Harvard Graduate School of Education.*

This chapter provides an accounting of the changing landscape higher education faces on the brink of the new millennium and how, through a visionary president and two key appointments, one university created a revitalized organization.

Redefining a University's Approach to Continuing Education (and Transforming Itself in the Process)

Bill G. Clutter

Pace University is a comprehensive, independent urban and suburban New York institution of higher education offering a wide range of academic and professional programs at the undergraduate and graduate levels through its six colleges and schools. It is today a university with more than fourteen thousand students enrolled in credit-bearing courses and certificate and degree programs.

By most measures, Pace University would be considered a very conservative institution, especially insofar as its continuing education and outreach activities are concerned. Each college or school is empowered to develop and deliver continuing professional education where content is linked to college curricula. Through these noncredit and nontraditional programs it is estimated that another five thousand individuals are served through the colleges and schools of Pace University.

It was not always so. Pace was founded in 1906 by two brothers, Homer and Charles Pace, as a business school for men and women who aspired to a better life. Pace Institute (as it was then known) became the premier accounting and business school for metropolitan New York City. In this earlier era the Pace Institute was recognized as an exemplary business school preparing its graduates for immediate employment in careers that offered growth and advancement and job security. Had it continued in that vein, it would today be viewed as a world-class professional school of accounting with its own well-regarded niche in that particular market in New York and the Northeast region.

Some forty-two years after its opening, Pace began its transformation into a modern university, with emphasis on the liberal arts and sciences, by developing a college of arts and sciences as both an autonomous academic unit and a foundation for the undergraduate core curriculum. The schools of nursing, law, education, and computer science and information systems were more recent responses to the needs of the New York City and Westchester communities for strong professional schools to prepare a well-educated workforce. It was through these platforms that the university maintained its aggressiveness toward serving new clientele, especially first-time college goers, recent immigrants, returning adults and veterans (World War II, Korea, and eventually Vietnam). It was also in this context that in 1976 the university established its University College, through which it conducted its universitywide outreach activities and developed and delivered uniquely adult education programs and degrees at times and locations convenient to the growing nontraditional student cohorts who had been flocking to higher education since the 1950s.

University College, serving as a gateway for the nontraditional adult students, complemented the other Pace colleges and schools that were imposing increasingly rigorous standards for admission and graduation in order to compete successfully with the more established and traditional higher education institutions of New York City. Meanwhile, the university continued its expansion, not only by adding schools and programs but by expanding its geographical reach. It established a foothold in Westchester County and along the way subsumed the College of White Plains, Briarcliff College, and some specialized two-year programs of Bennett College, en route to becoming the largest private university in that prosperous and growing county. Pace also became the first New York City university to recognize the significant midtown market and opened its Midtown Center in 1975, years before the establishment of the New York University (NYU) or City University of New York (CUNY) centers. Programs were offered throughout the boroughs, usually on-site at business, government, and not-for-profit organization locations. By the mid-1980s, Pace University had become one of the largest private universities in the state of New York and in the country, with more than thirty thousand students.

In 1984 Edward Mortola, the longtime president who had led the university through its halcyon days of growth, expansion, and changing mission, retired. His strong leadership was followed by an "internal" caretaker-manager president. This president held office for only six years but during a very critical period, which witnessed a vastly changing economy; massive investment by the state and federal government in the state and city higher education system, including the maturing public community college system; and more competitive leadership and expansion at the leading private institutions in the region, particularly at NYU, where John Brademas took the helm as president, and at Fordham University, which opened its beautiful new campus in the heart of the cultural district of Manhattan. Meanwhile, Pace University was standing still and tacitly pulling back and constricting its outreach, therein subtly but assuredly compromising its earlier successes.

In the leadership vacuum after Mortola, power and authority became more decentralized and the college and school deans, along with other universitywide administrators, made decisions that would have a major impact on Pace University's market position. There was an assumption that the university outreach activity under the direction and leadership of University College was undermining the effort among the colleges to raise standards. Rather than embrace its large outreach unit, Pace opted to close down University College and reassign the continuing education and outreach mission to the colleges and schools. That act also eliminated the adult-friendly degrees and open admission policies that had characterized the University College mission, replacing them with college- or school-based adult degree programs that, in fact, mirrored the more traditional degree programs but were offered part-time during the evenings. The weekend programs, intersession, and other nontraditional platforms died a natural death. The college-based and school-based noncredit offerings were for the most part designed to meet continuing professional education requirements or certification for the professions served, such as nursing, law, and business.

In short, this highly market-driven, aggressive, innovative university that had created markets and established a unique niche in the highly competitive metropolitan New York landscape suddenly and dramatically retreated and became, by choice, among the most "conservative" higher education institutions in the region. And with the expected results: the university's part-time enrollment began to decline precipitously, particularly at the undergraduate levels at a time when this was the fastest-growing student cohort at universities and colleges throughout the country; the noncredit continuing education offerings became very standard and college-specific and even these were limited. Not surprisingly, as competition for full-time traditional enrollments became more pronounced Pace began to lose enrollment in its full-time undergraduate cohort. Residence halls on the campus in Pleasantville were unfilled, and residence floors on the New York campus were converted to administrative offices.

The strong enrollments of the 1970s and 1980s that had provided and sustained the financial base to expand and maintain balanced budgets and financial vigor suddenly began to erode. As an institution with an enrollment-driven revenue base, tuition was increased to meet the escalating costs of higher education. This was the situation that the new president faced when she arrived on the scene in 1990.

Ushering in Bold Leadership and Creative Management

Patricia Ewers was the first externally selected president to lead Pace. Ewers hailed from De Paul University, where she had served her entire working career—as faculty member, department chair, dean, and ultimately vice president and dean of faculties. She had presided over De Paul, which resembled Pace during its heyday and included many of the same academic schools but wisely retained and even enriched its School for New Learning that reached out to adults. One of Ewers's first acts at Pace was to introduce a strategic planning process that resulted in some additional downsizing, most of it affecting the Westchester operations. She was intent on recapturing full-time undergraduate enrollment and filling the empty beds in the residence halls on the Westchester campus. She brought in an outside marketing organization to begin the process of repositioning Pace within its natural peer cohort of schools, and she quickly moved to staunch the hemorrhaging enrollment declines among traditional students.

There were so many organizational problems within the university structure that the outreach and continuing education (CE) issues and reversing the decline in adult, nontraditional students initially took a back seat. Indeed, as part of a universitywide restructuring, the undergraduate programs in the Westchester campus were consolidated on the Pleasantville-Briarcliff campus, and this led to even further declines among adult degree-seeking students. Thus, the university gave up its prime location in the populous city of White Plains—with its good public transportation system and its position as the seat of government, banking, commerce, and industry for Westchester County—as a venue for undergraduate adult degree programs. And adult students simply found the commute out to the "pastoral" Pleasantville campus to be inconvenient, if not downright impossible.

In 1995, after a series of resignations and reassignments, Ewers began a reorganization of the administration. She took that opportunity to combine two vice presidencies into one vice president for enrollment management and student life. The appointment of Philomena Mantella to head up this unit was a propitious one. Mantella called on a former colleague to assist with the development of a position paper to create an office of Adult, International, and Outreach Programs and Services (AIOPS) to be headed by an executive director. The position paper recognized the colleges and schools as both developer and deliverer of college- and school-based continuing education offerings, but at the same time pointed out the need for a centralized infrastructure to support these efforts through universitywide management and administration of registrar, bursar, marketing, and advertising activities, and especially in the development, consolidation, and maintenance of up-to-date databases for university use. In short, the new organization would provide a professionalism, standards, and continuity that was lacking in the highly decentralized Pace environment. With assurances all around, but amid some underlying skepticism and concern, the new organization took life in late 1995 with the appointment of the executive director and with the mission described earlier. The stage was set. The players were these: a dynamic president just embarking on her second five-year term and a new vice president of enrollment management and student life—armed with a philosophy and a plan to reshape if not transform the university's capacity to respond effectively to the nontraditional markets that represent the largest cohort of enrollments in today's higher education enterprise—and an experienced, professional, continuing education director—able, forward-thinking, risk-taking—ready to lead the charge and seeing the mission as critical to a private independent university that was trying to recapture market share, identify and respond to revenue opportunities, and reposition itself among its university peers in the highly competitive New York City market.

Putting the Plan into Practice

Decisions at the outset had a great impact on ensuring that the new AIOPS office would become an important feature in the operations at Pace University. First was the organization itself—an amalgam of administrators drawn from various units within the university—adult enrollment services from enrollment marketing and management; international student development from the Offices of Student Life; outreach from the admissions-adult enrollment services offices; and the English Language Institute from the vice president for academic affairs. Because these units retained existing responsibilities, each enjoyed instant visibility and credibility among the colleges and schools and the university at large.

The first task was to avoid any internal competition between AIOPS and the colleges and schools and their existing CE programs. It was agreed that AIOPS would not undertake noncredit program development and delivery without first offering the opportunity to the appropriate academic unit. If an opportunity were offered and rejected, then AIOPS would be permitted to deliver the program. AIOPS would also serve as a centralized marketing unit for the existing CE units—to create, manage, and refine databases; interface with university marketing offices in order to develop and maintain a common and consistent image in publications and advertising; and expand opportunities for cross-marketing. Finally, there was the pressing need to develop a standard for record keeping and fiscal reporting for the noncredit continuing education activities offered throughout the university. This would be achieved through the adoption of a centralized registration and record-keeping system and through a general standardization of financial reports, policies, and procedures for revenue sharing.

After a lengthy process, a set of policies and procedures were developed outlining these concepts and issues in a way that confirmed the colleges and schools as the primary program delivery system while AIOPS made moves to take on more of the centralized administrative tasks and functions.

The Midtown Center

Meanwhile, other events were taking shape that would have even greater impact on the positioning of this office. First, the executive council of the university, made up of the president and the vice presidents, had been considering for more than a year the disposition of the Midtown Center, which had been leased almost twenty years previously, during the peak of Pace's expansion. The facility, which was very outdated and limited in its use to evening credit instruction at the undergraduate and graduate levels, was home to the master of science degree in publishing—an obvious choice of location for this midtown-based industry. It also served as the site for a Pace Computer Learning Center operation, the venue for noncredit delivery of computer software and related classes. The president had in hand a report prepared by a committee chaired by the chief financial officer simply to let the lease expire in March 1996 and give up the midtown presence. Based on scant survey data and mostly anecdotal information, the report suggested that the university would not suffer any loss of enrollments and that all those who attended Midtown would commute to the downtown campus some fifty blocks away by subway. The report also concluded that there would be ample space at the downtown campus to accommodate the courses offered in the twenty-five classrooms at Midtown, plus house the master's in publishing program and the Pace Computer Learning Center.

In a move that propelled the office of AIOPS into a highly visible role and the center of decision making as it pertained to university outreach and continuing education at Pace, the president called on the executive director to chair a new committee to review the status of the Midtown Center. This move reflected her growing unease with the conclusions drawn by the earlier committee and its report. Based perhaps on intuition, or her own experience in adult outreach or, even more likely, the recent history at Westchester—where her decision to discontinue undergraduate instruction at the White Plains campus had resulted in a precipitous decline in adult enrollment in that county—the president was clearly not comfortable with the recommendation to close the Midtown Center. She asked the new committee to conduct its work and have a formal report on her desk within one month.

The recommendations of this committee were dramatically different from those reported by the earlier committee; namely, giving up the midtown presence would be disastrous in terms of loss of students and would seriously jeopardize the master's in publishing program. Furthermore, there would be no equivalent space on the downtown campus to house a dedicated program such as the Pace Computer Learning Center, and it was highly unlikely that the crowded evening program at the downtown campus could accommodate the many open-enrollment graduate and undergraduate courses and some noncredit courses that were scheduled each semester, including the summer sessions, at Midtown. The single advantage to be gained by closing the Midtown Center would be eliminating the monthly lease payment and related expenses. This benefit, however, would be more than offset by the loss of revenue from enrollments, even in the unlikely event that all or most of the students currently served at the midtown location would transfer to the downtown campus. A comprehensive financial audit that segregated and identified all income and expense associated with the midtown operation confirmed that the return on investment for the space far exceeded that for the main campus.

The report was accepted in its entirety. The executive director of AIOPS was given the responsibility to begin at once either to renegotiate the lease for the existing center—incorporating major upgrades so that it would have use as a corporate training site during normal business hours, an expanded and enhanced computer learning center, and a dedicated multimedia laboratory to support and enhance the master's in publishing program—or to explore other locations that could accommodate the desired classroom and laboratory configurations and provide a state-of-the-art training facility for Pace in a midtown location. Choosing the second option, a new facility was leased in a landmark building a block away from the original site and, importantly, in walking distance from Grand Central Station, the most important transportation hub in Manhattan. Pace also took advantage of the "grand opening" of the new venue to promote corporate outreach for the university and establish a "centralized" university outreach presence at the new center through the appointment of a director of corporate outreach and university extension, who reported to the executive director of AIOPS.

The timing of the new lease also was in Pace University's favor. Because of the prevailing real estate market, the space was leased for almost $20 per square foot less than the former space, and 75 percent of the costs of the $2.3 million buildout were handled by the building owner. Every semester since opening (beginning with spring 1997) has shown a double-digit increase in enrollment over the previous corresponding semester; that is, spring to spring, summer to summer, and fall to fall. The business school's executive MBA program has been relocated to the center to take advantage of its corporate look, furnishings, and prime location. The income and enrollments for the Pace Computer Learning Center have almost doubled as a result of its expanded capacity and new professional setting.

A New Strategic Agenda for the New Millennium

In February 1996, President Ewers formed her Strategic Agenda Steering Committee. Some of the predominant themes to emerge related to globalism and internationalism—focusing on the intensive study of languages and the students' need to have competence in at least one language other than their own native language; curriculum issues that would deal with an understanding of global systems, including the dynamics of the international economy; development of problem-focused programs of study that are more practical than theoretical and oriented around problems in the real world; the need to make international education more democratic and universal, giving all undergraduates exposure to other peoples, languages, and cultures; and the recognition of the cultural diversity of the United States. Other issues that emerged were lifetime learning and "just-in-time" learning. A third theme dealt with the expanding role of technology in development and delivery of education and training. A fourth recognized a trend toward establishing partners and alliances that permit institutions to maximize resources and avoid or reduce duplication. The work of this committee continued nonstop for more than two years. A final report incorporating the new agenda for the new millennium was approved by the committee and submitted to the various constituencies of the university. It still has not been formally approved, but it already serves as the basis for institutional planning and budgeting.

As the new director of AIOPS was settling into the new position, an inconspicuous announcement in *The New York Times* would present another unique opportunity.

The World Trade Institute

In February 1996, a notification issued by the Port Authority of New York and New Jersey solicited proposals for the purchase of the World Trade Institute (WTI) and the Port Authority library. The World Trade Institute was a well-known institution in New York City that had program reach through seminars that took it to as many as twenty-nine cities across the United States and international training programs that took it to all parts of the world. The WTI language center offered business-oriented language instruction in ten languages and English as a second language for nonnative speakers, whereas the forty-five-year-old Evening School of World Trade served as the principal source of hands-on, thorough, and practical training in import, export, freight forwarding, and customs brokerage. The evening school had also partnered with several universities, so that evening-school courses could be used to meet degree requirements for a major with an international orientation. Finally, the institute itself included a full floor at One World Trade Center that was custom-designed to serve as a world-class conference center, with incomparable views and services.

With the full support of the president, the executive council, and the board of trustees, Pace responded to the request for proposal (RFP). This proposal was well received and ultimately accepted by the Port Authority in May, and the actual transfer took place on July 1, 1997.

With the stroke of a pen, AIOPS, a universitywide operation with limited programming responsibility and authority (the English Language Institute and two continuing professional education certification programs), in existence for little more than a year, was transformed into the largest continuing education unit in Pace University, with a mission that touched most if not all of the academic units that make up the university.

Conclusion

Under the thoughtful and bold leadership of its president, Pace University made a series of strategic and critical decisions to reposition itself during that president's second and final term of office: the establishment of the Office of Adult, International, and Outreach Programs and Services; the identification and employment of an entrepreneurial advocate to head the office and provide an organizational framework to fulfill the promise of an expanded mission and strategic agenda; the decision to remain in midtown and reinvest in the operation; and ultimately the decision to acquire the World Trade Institute. As a result, Pace will emerge as an institution that is totally committed to a twenty-first century agenda: internationalism, technology, teaching and learning across the lifetime, meeting the needs of adults and nontraditional students, and reinventing curriculum and service to mesh with the societal and economic needs of the populace.

Pace has embarked on a bold course to make continuing education a legitimate child of the academy rather than a stepchild. Mutual respect between the professional adult learner and the academic environment is a powerful element in encouraging people to pursue further education, lifelong learning, and new ideas. In order to survive economically, the academy must become more relevant to the majority of the population. The university of the twenty-first century will no longer survive as an ivory tower, alienated from real life; on the contrary, its synergies with the professional world and its responsiveness to the needs of working adults will help expand its reach and enrich its resources. Diversifying the audience entails more work for the university staff, both academic and administrative, but its rewards are greater still. By removing the traditional boundaries between the world of theory with that of practice, the university returns to the Greek ideal of education: knowledge as the vehicle to meaningful participation in society.

Transformation, creativity, luck, timing, leadership, vision, hard work—all are key elements that have played significant roles in the reengineering of Pace University. We've taken only the first steps and made the first commitments, but our direction is firmly established and will not be deterred.

BILL G. CLUTTER is the executive director of the Office of Adult, International, and Outreach Programs and Services and of the World Trade Institute at Pace University in New York.

The Bell Atlantic Corporation has entered into an agreement with a consortium of community colleges in the Northeast for the purpose of offering an associate degree in applied science with a telecommunications concentration. The program, called NEXT STEP, is offered to Bell Atlantic employees during their workday. This specially designed degree program allows for a creative partnership between education, labor, and industry.

Creating Innovative Partnerships

James F. Polo, Louise M. Rotchford, Paula M. Setteducati

The more we share an idea, the more valuable it becomes.
—Raymond Smith

Teamwork and cooperation was the message presented by Raymond Smith, chief executive officer of Bell Atlantic, at a recent Long Island college commencement. Smith told the graduates that Bell Atlantic was now embracing both knowledge and teamwork as critical educational goals. Achieving those goals was going to be pivotal to the implementation of a newly fashioned corporate strategy that would result in an employee who would more readily fit into the workplace of the twenty-first century.

A New Model of Education

With his graduation-day comments, Smith challenged all educators to enter into completely new and unfamiliar territory and begin to work more closely with business to design degree and training programs that would be beneficial to students, business, and educational institutions. Specifically, he asked the faculty and administration of today's institutions to discard the old model of education that stressed individualism—working, studying, and learning alone—and pioneer a new model of education. This new way of teaching and learning would stress the value of technological competence coupled with a specific grouping of core competencies designed to produce

Note: We wish to acknowledge Arlene Beauchemin, human resources staff director at Bell Atlantic, for providing us with the NYNEX in-house articles shown in the References, all of which she edited or contributed to.

a new and different graduate. A graduate who, Smith hoped, would be more equipped to become the "supertechnician" of the future, proficient in the technology of the industry, and fluent enough in the teamwork aspects of the workplace to solve new and unforeseen problems. In support of this vision, John Abeles, acting vice president for training and education at Bell Atlantic, recently suggested that modern education should discard the old model of learning, which puts a premium on the rote learning of facts, and replace it with a new model that stresses the value of lifelong learning.

We in the community colleges are often asked to respond to the educational challenges of the communities that surround and support us, to design and implement new and innovative programs to our various constituent communities. However, as educators we must be diligent in protecting the integrity of the curriculum. The value of the degrees we grant and the excellence of the training we provide must be of paramount concern. New program models must be scrutinized to ensure that they meet the highest criteria that we as professional educators can realistically set. The vision of Smith and Abeles is currently being realized on twenty-two community and technical college campuses throughout the Northeast. It is Bell Atlantic's unique partnership, known as NEXT STEP.

NEXT STEP

The NEXT STEP program is an educational model designed to achieve Bell Atlantic's goals by training employees to become the workforce mandated for the future. It is a corporate-sponsored associate degree program that is intended to graduate technically proficient workers who have also been trained in the art of working together. This chapter discusses some of the impact, problems, and concerns that have been experienced with the adoption of the NEXT STEP program at Nassau Community College. It also points out many of the new ideas, programs, and teamwork initiatives implemented by the staff of the Office of Community Services at this institution.

Bell Atlantic's NEXT STEP program was conceived to be a different curriculum offered through a familiar delivery system. In 1995, Bell Atlantic (formerly NYNEX) solicited help from a consortium of community colleges in New York State, led by Hudson Valley Community College (HVCC) in Troy, New York, to provide a curriculum that would lead to a new and different degree. This was a large-scale undertaking because the focus of the program was new, the curriculum needed to be written and adopted by all the participating community college faculties, and it also needed the approval of the New York State Education Department. Embedded within the degree program—from the written curriculum, to the hidden curriculum, to the methodology of how it was to be taught—was an outline of core competencies designed to facilitate the goals of Bell Atlantic and presumably the rest of the telecommunications industry. The recipients of the degree were to become the "communications technicians of the future," meaning that they were to be trained to become a cadre of well-educated technicians exposed to engineering concepts, computer training, the soft skills necessary to deal with corporate customers, and the teamwork skills necessary to work in large groups to accomplish predetermined tasks. What Bell Atlantic was asking for was not only curricular change but also culture change.

Program Background. "Given the pace and complexity of technological change within the industry and the requirement not only to improve productivity but also to deliver quality, variety, customization, convenience and timeliness for customers, businesses have come to grips with the necessity of investing in the competence and expertise of the workforce as a critical strategy to ensure the needed flexibility to compete successfully in the future," reads the NEXT STEP program's 1995–96 strategic plan (*Corporate University Xchange*, 1996).

When NYNEX chairman Ivan Seidenberg first envisioned the NEXT STEP program in 1994, he realized that updating employee skills would allow the company to retain workers and ensure that NYNEX was ready for the challenges of the twenty-first century (*FOTEP News*, 1996). If his vision was realized, the company would remain competitive through an enlightened and changed workforce equipped with cutting-edge skills to handle the company's ever-changing state-of-the-art technologies, the autonomy to meet customer demands, and a lifelong willingness to learn. This was a dramatic shift—from the training push of the eighties to the learning philosophy of the nineties. As Abeles stated, "Technologies will change, but the competencies associated with lifelong learning will serve employees long into the future" (*Corporate University Xchange*, 1996).

This unprecedented undertaking would make NYNEX workers the best educated in the telecommunications industry. In order to accomplish this goal, there needed to be a dramatic paradigm shift both for NYNEX and eventually for all twenty-two colleges presently involved in the NEXT STEP program, including Nassau Community College.

Creation of NEXT STEP. NEXT STEP is part of the NYNEX University concept, which was a development of the 1994 bargaining agreements between NYNEX and its unions, Communications Workers of America (CWA) and the International Brotherhood of Electrical Workers (IBEW). In this groundbreaking partnership, NYNEX, CWA, and IBEW established collaboration with community and technical colleges throughout the Northeast to restructure the various existing technical degree programs to meet the demands of all members. The result was the NEXT STEP program, an associate degree in applied science with a focus on telecommunications technology. To ensure that the degree would be uniform across all colleges, the curriculum would include sixty credits: twenty from a traditional liberal arts curriculum, twenty from telecommunications courses, and twenty from electric and electronics courses. In addition to the degree-specific curriculum, all parties agreed to include certain customer-focused core competencies in each course, such as teamwork, customer service, leadership, quality, problem solving, and technical and service delivery. These are now referred to as the *umbrella competencies*. NYNEX provided technological expertise to the curriculum development effort and assisted with the selection of software applications that would be used to enrich laboratory experiments. Lotus Notes, an e-mail program used throughout the company, was incorporated into the program and introduced in the computer applications course. According to NYNEX administration, the purpose of the inclusion of Lotus Notes was to create a virtual community of continuous learners inside and beyond the classroom.

NEXT STEP was piloted on six community college campuses within New York State in spring 1995 with a total of 180 students. Nassau Community College was chosen as one of the pilot colleges with 25 students. Today, in place for four years and anticipating its first graduates in January 1999, the program boasts 1,360 students attending twenty-two community and technical colleges in New York and New England. Selection is by seniority and the ability to pass college entrance tests. Students must also fulfill a host of college and company requirements.

Participants attend school one day per week on company time during two fifteen-week semesters per year. Like any other college students, NEXT STEP students are required to complete homework assignments and team projects. These assignments usually add an additional twenty hours to their school week. The company pays all costs involved—tuition, books, lab fees, and so on. All NEXT STEP students, faculty, and program staff are also provided with laptop computers, and calculators are provided to all students and math instructors. Calculators and laptops are essential tools for the program. Using laptops in class and for assignments addresses a number of program goals: *Goal One:* students learn and use new technology; *Goal Two:* faculty model the use of new technology; *Goal Three:* new instructional and learning methodologies are developed to change how teachers teach and how students learn; and *Goal Four:* collaboration and communication among the various learning groups—student-student, student-faculty, faculty-faculty—is facilitated.

Creativity and the NEXT STEP Program

The NEXT STEP program is creative and innovative in many different ways. Prominent are the following:

Curriculum-Instruction. NEXT STEP is a specific degree program customized to meet Bell Atlantic's corporate needs. It uses a consistent curriculum shared by all participating colleges. Embedded in the curriculum is the use of Lotus Notes and the umbrella competencies that the corporation mandates. Students and faculty are encouraged to use Lotus Notes as a primary means of communication throughout their course work. The program uses new instructional techniques, including more student participation, more hands-on learning, and fewer lecture formats. Another hallmark of NEXT STEP is the collaborative learning approach. Different departments have been involved in partnering projects to facilitate transference of skills from one class to another.

Consortium. NEXT STEP consists of twenty-two schools in consortium, of which the lead school is HVCC, which was chosen by Bell Atlantic to coordinate the project. It is also a creative partnership consisting of education, business, and labor that was cited by former Secretary of Labor Robert Reich as a model program.

Administration. The NEXT STEP program makes certain administrative adjustments mandatory. Because students are released from their work duties for only one day each week, courses must be block-scheduled to accommodate two four-hour classes.

The program also must build in flexible scheduling to accommodate the vagaries of weather that Bell Atlantic is forced to respond to. For example, in times of weather emergency, Bell Atlantic may request that the start of a semester be delayed or classes canceled while their employees are deployed to areas as needed.

Another adjustment colleges must make involves the college entrance procedure and testing requirement. Each participating college must use the ASSET (Assessment of Skills of Successful Entry and Transfer [American College Testing Program, 1993]) test for program admission and eligibility, regardless of the testing requirements mainstream students are asked to fulfill. Another interesting departure for the NEXT STEP program is grade disclosure. Students must sign a release so that colleges can report grades to the lead school, HVCC. The program has a strict grading policy: students must maintain a 2.0 grade point average (GPA), and a failing grade in any course is reason for dismissal from NEXT STEP. Students and faculty are asked to evaluate courses they are involved in, and the data are used to help in a continuous improvement process review. HVCC and Bell Atlantic conduct end-of-year surveys of both student and faculty satisfaction and reactions. Results are used to plan the agenda of a yearly Faculty Institute, which is attended by hundreds of NEXT STEP staff, faculty, and students.

The Impact of NEXT STEP on Nassau Community College

The Bell Atlantic NEXT STEP program has been a very positive addition to the community services office of Nassau Community College, and it has been responsible for a number of changes that have had a most beneficial impact on the office's staff outlook, typical course programming, and standard administrative procedures. The addition of the NEXT STEP program to other, more usual areas of responsibility has helped all community services staff to think creatively and to welcome the addition of new ventures to our roster of responsibilities.

Evolution of the Program: Reacting to Need. In the early stages of the program at Nassau, administrative responsibilities for NEXT STEP were housed in the engineering department. For a variety of reasons, in August 1996 the vice president for academic affairs shifted administrative duties for the program to the Office of Community Services. By this time, three semesters had passed, the curriculum had already been agreed to, and most policies and procedures had already been established. Nevertheless, the Office of Community Services eagerly accepted the challenge and responsibilities that this new assignment held.

At Nassau, the Office of Community Services consists of the areas of continuing education (noncredit adult education programming); special programs for business (noncredit contract training for local companies and corporations); the Drinking Driver Program (New York State–mandated classroom training program for motorists who have been arrested for drinking and driving); and the extension site program (credit courses in local high schools and libraries that are aimed at traditional and nontraditional college students). The addition of the NEXT STEP program necessitated that the college add support staff, administration, and budget resource dollars to facilitate the new scope of responsibility. Specifically, the college would be forced to add a new responsibility center to community services—the Center for Corporate Credit Programming.

When NEXT STEP was first assigned to community services, it was cause for much reflection and concern among all the professional staff. For anyone who has worked in educational administration for even a brief period, the standard mantra is to try to "accomplish more with less." Each time a new responsibility is added, the fear of not being able to meet objectives is gripping, as valuable resources are often already strained to the limit. Although the tuition revenue from the program promised to be substantial and there was a modest administrative component added in to help defray costs, the college faced the problem of funding a new responsibility center, and a full commitment for administrative and clerical support would be crucial. We needed to hire a full-time person with support staff to help ensure that NEXT STEP was run to the satisfaction of the management team at Bell Atlantic, the lead community college team from Hudson Valley Community College, the students, and the college faculty. We were fortunate to find and hire a transitional part-time person who had a great deal of experience in noncredit programming, credit programming, and grant work. She was assigned work exclusively on the NEXT STEP project while a full-time position could be created, a search performed, and the position permanently filled.

Benefits to Nassau. With the assignment of NEXT STEP to community services, a number of benefits immediately were realized.

New Relationships with Other College Departments. An important link was established with a number of college departments, links that heretofore had been attempted but never fully realized. Because of the pivotal nature of the NEXT STEP program, our new part-time coordinator was put in the enviable position of working directly with the admissions office, the registrar's office, the student financial affairs office, the English department, the mathematics and computer science department, the engineering and physics department, the academic computer services office, and the testing office.

New Staff. In order to service our new clientele properly, the hiring of new staff was in order. Once the part-time project coordinator was in place, one of the first problems that surfaced was that of providing support services for the laptop computers that Bell Atlantic provided to each participant. Laptops are convenient but do have some reliability problems, and students were reporting many of the expected problems to the program coordinator. A part-time technical assistant was hired to support the software and hardware problems encountered. This was critical because students were required to use their laptops extensively for homework and team projects, and they needed to be assured of a rapid response to their difficulty.

Tutoring. The difficulty of the courses, coupled with the uneven preparation of some of the students, indicated a need for academic support by many of the NEXT STEP students. Some of them had been out of high school for over twenty-five years, and they were encountering much difficulty with the technical math requirements of the program. With the support of the vice president for academic affairs, the college expended funds for a tutoring program designed to enhance the academic success of those who were having difficulty. Course professors were hired to provide formal extra-help sessions to students who were having problems. Extra-help sessions were carefully timed to occur during lunch hour and after the workday.

New Full-Time Coordinator. A full-time coordinator was hired to oversee the program, intervene in problems before they grew, and plan for new corporate programs for the future.

New Procedures and Activities. Some of the steps taken for addressing NEXT STEP program problems led to the establishment of new procedures and new activities for community services staff.

Community Services Newsletter. The intricacies of NEXT STEP necessitated a mechanism to disseminate information pertinent to the program participants and the college community at large. Frequent meetings between the program coordinator, interested faculty, and department chairs were scheduled and held. Further, it was decided that one of the best ways to disseminate information was to establish a newsletter that would be published a few times each semester to "get the word out" to the college community about all programs run through community services.

New Corporate Program Initiatives. The success of NEXT STEP illustrated the ability of the college to partner with business to educate and train employees, and the program served as a model of corporate and educational sharing. Community services is actively exploring partnerships with local business and industry, and several recent programs with local business are being explored for rejuvenation.

New Initiatives with Governmental Agencies. Building on newly learned skills and the success of NEXT STEP, the Office of Community Services recently embarked on a number of new partnerships with the Nassau County

Department of Social Services to provide both credit and noncredit programs to their clientele.

New Focus on Programs for Business and Industry. Community services now markets and sells training programs to local business and industry via a focus on the greater benefit of linking into the college's comprehensive services in credit and noncredit areas. This multiple-offering approach has proven successful with local business and industry.

New Generic Telecommunications Degree Program. The success of the Bell Atlantic NEXT STEP program has facilitated the initiation of a new generic associate degree in telecommunications technology for interested students who are not employed by Bell Atlantic, or for those who are employed by Bell Atlantic but do not meet company criteria for admission to NEXT STEP. This generic program combines the elements of an electronics technology program with specific courses in telecommunications and prepares students for careers in computer communications, switching, voice and data, cellular, field service, product development, and system troubleshooting.

Faculty Trained in Advanced Technologies. The NEXT STEP program has brought with it a wealth of opportunities for Nassau Community College faculty members. In particular, during Bell Atlantic–sponsored Faculty Institutes, where faculty members design course curricula, faculty members are introduced to state-of-the-art telecommunication technologies. Demonstrations of these new technologies provide faculty members with increased knowledge to share with their students and greater insight into how academia can support the corporate environment.

New Noncredit Opportunities. Shortly after embarking on the NEXT STEP program, it became apparent that Nassau Community College's opportunities to provide instruction to Bell Atlantic employees were not limited to the credit environment. Short-term, noncredit training opportunities quickly emerged to help support the existing credit programming. Because many of the initial applicants found themselves failing admissions testing, thirty-six-hour noncredit brush-up courses in algebra were designed and delivered to help remediate them. On successful completion of the course, participants were allowed to retest for admission.

Noncredit training opportunities also emerged in the area of computers. To help support and encourage NEXT STEP students to use Lotus Notes on a regular basis, Nassau Community College provided enhanced Lotus Notes training during students' vacation between semesters.

Statistics and Success Rates

At the Faculty Institute held at Hudson Valley Community College in June 1998, the following statistics and success rates were shared among program participants and providers:

- Fifty-three percent of NEXT STEP students have a 3.5 or higher GPA.

- According to Bell Atlantic, the program attrition rate is 33 percent, which, as was pointed out, is no larger than for other, similar college programs.

Bell Atlantic surveys show these averages:

- The student survey found that 72 percent of students rated the instructors' ability to create a learning environment very good or excellent, 88 percent of students used their laptop as part of their course work each semester, 68 percent of students rated the program overall very good or excellent, and 60 percent of students felt that instructors were successful in incorporating umbrella competencies in their classrooms.
- The faculty survey found that almost 78 percent rated their experience using computers in their course as very good or excellent, 92 percent rated their experience in teaching their NEXT STEP students as very good or excellent, 56 percent rated their experience in using Lotus Notes as very good or excellent, and 69 percent reported that they do include umbrella competencies in the course curriculum.

Conclusion

As stated earlier, the NEXT STEP program has been a positive experience for Nassau and particularly for the Office of Community Services. Before our involvement with this program, community services simply dealt with non-credit training programs, which carry little prestige among colleagues. As we grew in experience with the administration of the program, we also grew in stature with our colleagues. As stated throughout this chapter, new initiatives and relationships naturally sprung from the interaction of our staff with the various academic and support service departments.

The NEXT STEP program has proven to be a win-win innovative project for Bell Atlantic, labor, the participating colleges, and the students. Bell Atlantic has achieved its goals by initiating a customized college-level degree program for its employees, who are learning state-of-the-art telecommunications skills as well as the umbrella competencies. The NEXT STEP experience should place them in leadership roles throughout the telecommunications industry for many years to come. As for labor, its members are obtaining a new level of technical competence and confidence that will make them a more valuable commodity at Bell Atlantic or any other telecommunications company. As for the colleges, NEXT STEP has provided numerous opportunities for growth and reflection. Faculty members have been afforded opportunities to hone their teaching skills to new populations of corporate customers, learn the cutting-edge technology of the telecommunications field, and use the computer as a communications and instructional tool.

The Office of Community Services was provided with an opportunity that was unparalleled in potential. In just a short period of time, we have been inspired to provide new programs in new formats for new populations. We have developed new competencies in line with the umbrella competencies embedded in NEXT STEP. There is a growing emphasis on teamwork, sharing information, developing leadership skills, and problem solving. As anticipated in the NEXT STEP curriculum, educators should become models, and the staff of community services is working toward that goal.

References

Corporate University Xchange, Mar.-Apr. 1996, *VII* (2).
FOTEP NEWS, Oct. 1996, p. 3.

JAMES F. POLO is dean for continuing education and community services at Nassau Community College, Garden City, New York.

LOUISE M. ROTCHFORD is assistant dean for community services and director of special programs for business at Nassau Community College, Garden City, New York.

PAULA M. SETTEDUCATI is coordinator of NEXT STEP at Nassau Community College, Garden City, New York.

Universities operating in a knowledge-based economy must approach problem solving using interdisciplinary and cross-professional perspectives.

Dialogue and Collaboration as Keys to Building Innovative Educational Initiatives in a Knowledge-Based Economy

Mary Lindenstein Walshok

As an early baby boomer, I grew up in a middle-class America of heroes and geniuses. Whether it was "The Lone Ranger" on television, *The Loneliness of the Long Distance Runner* (Sillitoe, 1992) in literature, the celebration of the whiz kids on the "Sixty-Four Thousand Dollar Question," or the fast-tracking of the especially able in the era of *Sputnik,* mine was a generation that prized individual achievement and genius. The culture of exceptionality that developed in this country after World War II was reinforced by our incredible achievements in science and technology during the Cold War. And it has shaped the popular view that creativity is a highly individualistic quality, that ability is a gift—as in programs for "gifted" students—and that creativity comes from "flashes of genius" rather than from social processes.

But in the new knowledge-based economy, characterized by digital (that is, networked processes) rather than analogic (that is, linear processes), creativity and innovation increasingly come from *webs of talent* rather than flashes of genius. In this chapter, I will describe how the development of institutional mechanisms capable of addressing emerging transdisciplinary knowledge needs in the new networked economy can give rise to innovative academic initiatives unlikely to emerge from the more linear, individual, expert models of knowledge development and dissemination characterizing most research universities.

NEW DIRECTIONS FOR ADULT AND CONTINUING EDUCATION, no. 81, Spring 1999 © Jossey-Bass Publishers

Why New Models of Innovation Are Needed

In a knowledge-based society, ever-changing economic, community, and individual learning challenges arise from rapid transformations in the technologies shaping industry and work processes as well as from the demographic and geopolitical forces affecting the daily activities of communities and citizens. The intersection of these myriad forces yields demands from society for access to knowledge that is multidisciplinary and integrative. In the context of the isolated disciplinary boundaries of universities, developing innovative programs that serve emerging needs is a formidable challenge. Nonetheless, it is a challenge that must and can be met. A few specific examples may be useful here.

At a recent meeting in Fresno, California, of the Governor's Economic Strategies Panel on which I serve, panelists were briefed during two days of testimony on the changing character of the Central Valley, often referred to as "the bread basket of the world." Issues affecting the future of agricultural productivity were discussed, as were the many ways in which advances in molecular biology and information technology, especially geographic information systems (GIS), were transforming an industry seeking to prosper in the new global economy. The deliberations of our panel have been informed by numerous briefings like this one around the state. Each has been structured around an analysis of how key economic clusters are affecting the prosperity of the state. This approach represents a new way to think about the economy. Rather than analyzing the future in terms of single variables, such as workforce trends inside a specific industry made up of a collection of firms or producers, *cluster analysis* (Porter, 1998) focuses on the full range of preproduction, supplier, production, postproduction, and community infrastructure capacities involved with any specific industry, from information technology to agriculture to tourism. The agricultural cluster map shown in Figure 8.1, which was presented at our meeting in Fresno, describes the range of activities, knowledge bases, and competencies associated with agriculture in the modern era. In its multidimensionality, the map highlights how complex and interdependent are the factors affecting any aspect of the industry.

One could develop similar maps for the tourism or transportation industries, or for health care or education, for that matter. What is critical from the point of view of this chapter is that the economic issues and social problems for which continuous access to knowledge and competency development are essential increasingly involve clusters of overlapping conditions and forms of expertise, rather than narrowly defined knowledge bases and skill sets. This is why the concept of webs of talent is so relevant. In order to address effectively the very dynamic leadership needs, the ever-changing technical competencies, or the evolving productivity challenges of an industry such as agriculture, curriculum developers need to draw on a much wider range of information resources. By not doing so, academic planners will continue to be vulnerable to the criticism by leadership in government, industry, and vital social institutions such as the schools, that the knowledge work of the academy is increasingly remote from

Figure 8.1. Agricultural Cluster Map

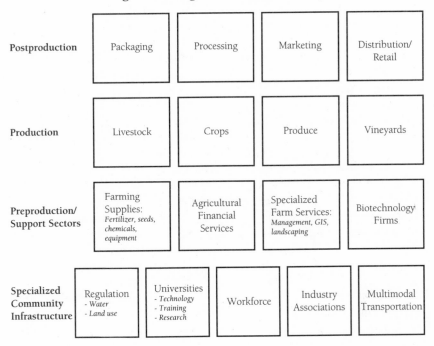

Postproduction	Packaging	Processing	Marketing	Distribution/ Retail
Production	Livestock	Crops	Produce	Vineyards
Preproduction/ Support Sectors	Farming Supplies: *Fertilizer, seeds, chemicals, equipment*	Agricultural Financial Services	Specialized Farm Services: *Management, GIS, landscaping*	Biotechnology Firms
Specialized Community Infrastructure	Regulation - Water - Land use	Universities - Technology - Training - Research	Workforce	Industry Associations	Multimodal Transportation

the knowledge needs of society. It is essential that all academic disciplines—not just engineering, professional schools, and the sciences—evaluate the models of creativity and innovation on which they rely.

It is often said that people and communities have problems, whereas universities have departments. Although this is a useful way to define the foregoing example, it's overly facile. Clearly, human and community issues connect to a variety of forces and must be understood from interdisciplinary perspectives. But increasingly, intellectual and scientific fields also are experiencing new forms of convergence. This point is compellingly argued in E. O. Wilson's article in the *Atlantic Monthly*, "Consilience," in which he asserts that the intellectual advances achieved through the growing specialization and fragmentation of disciplines in the modern era has reached the point of absurdity, with many physicists who don't "know what a gene is, and biologists who guess that string theory has something to do with violins" (1998, p. 56). Wilson suggests that at this point in the history of knowledge it is increasingly important to address those intellectual and real-world problems where multiple disciplines intersect, to move from "silos" of distinct expertise to concentric circles of overlapping knowledge.

Michael Gibbons, a leading British science policy analyst, argues in his book *The New Production of Knowledge* (1994) that both the state of knowledge in contemporary times as well as its growing value to diverse spheres of human endeavor is giving rise to a new form of knowledge production that he describes as highly dynamic, transdisciplinary, less reliant on single institutions (that is, universities) for expertise, and more socially accountable. The core of Gibbons's thesis is that "the parallel expansion in the number of potential knowledge producers on the supply side and the expansion of the requirement of specialist knowledge on the demand side are creating the conditions for the emergence of a new mode of knowledge production" (p. 13).

This evolving state of affairs has implications for all institutions with a stake in knowledge production, whether universities, research centers, or industrial laboratories. It requires a new approach to defining research questions as well as teaching and learning objectives. It calls on such skills as convening, conversing across disciplines, and ultimately building and energizing transdisciplinary teams. In such a knowledge universe, institutions and individuals capable of weaving these webs of talent and developing agendas that integrate diverse forms of knowledge that can be accessed and used by a variety of problem-solving communities will have the creative edge.

Example of Innovation by a Web of Talent

More than a decade ago, the chancellor of the University of California at San Diego was approached by the city's Economic Development Corporation (EDC) to explore how the university might more actively stimulate the entrepreneurial development of new companies, building on the large basic research productivity of the campus and related research institutes. The campus offered to look into how it might become an entrepreneurial resource to the wider community. Out of necessity, it had to develop an innovative response. The EDC had recommended a new degree program in entrepreneurship, but in the absence of a business school and faculty whose research or teaching interests at the time were focused on business or innovation, the person charged with developing an idea—myself—had to come up with something unique. Out of necessity, I solicited input from a cross section of UCSD academics, a variety of business service providers, and high-tech leaders working in the San Diego region. The process proved to be a highly creative one through which a number of ideas from initially very diverse sources converged into a concept for a unique program.

The concept that emerged—to create an interdisciplinary, cross-professional network of education and support—was uniquely suited to a research-intensive campus while still being responsive to regional economic development needs. It emphasized the special entrepreneurship characteristics necessary to support technology-based companies in contrast to general business entrepreneurship skills (to which a more traditional business school could contribute). In addition to targeting science and technology-driven companies, the concept emphasized reliance on practitioners and experienced high-tech entrepreneurs, given the youthful stage of the industry and the absence of a wide body of research and professional teaching expertise on technology entrepreneurship even in established business schools. Finally, as a result of a broadly consultative process, the program concept also emphasized frequent and mutually enriching interaction between scientists, engineers, and critical business service providers such as venture capitalists, attorneys, accountants, and marketing specialists as a way to enhance the competencies of all the partners in the business development process and build a sense of community (similar to that in Silicon Valley) among all the players in the high-tech business development process.

The working committee that was convened to develop an academic plan based on this three-pronged concept crossed every traditional boundary typical in a more mature (and fragmented) university campus. It included the extension dean (me) as the convener, a professor of materials science (recently appointed as the first dean of a newly formed division of engineering), the medical school dean, a venture capitalist, an accountant, an attorney, the head of the EDC, the CEO of a telecommunications company, and the CEO of a biotech company. Together, the group developed the UCSD Program in Technology & Entrepreneurship, later to be known as CONNECT. Today, the program is recognized around the world as an innovative "incubator without walls" that has facilitated the emergence of hundreds of high-tech firms, billions of dollars in external investment in San Diego companies, and the creation of sixty thousand new jobs in the region over the last decade.

CONNECT itself grew out of a process. It did not spring, full blown, from someone's head. In fact, the process was triggered by an idea that was undoable as spelled out. Nonetheless, it tapped into a "felt need" among a large, diverse community of knowledge and experience. By delving into that diverse community and drawing together some of the best regional thinkers and practitioners, a wholly new and innovative approach to developing entrepreneurship in the region emerged.

A small group of backers contributed modest funds to jump-start the effort; an experienced, successful retired entrepreneur with unprecedented energy and salesmanship was recruited to lead the program; and today CONNECT has 650 company members and an annual budget of $1.5 million and is stimulating parallel programs across the country and around the globe.

CONNECT's key activities today reflect its core commitment to building webs of talent, networking with all the partners in the business development process, and continually bridging academic and practitioner expertise in order to support individual entrepreneurs and nurture an entrepreneurial culture in the region. The varied CONNECT programs offer entrepreneurs the help they need to expand their companies. At the same time, CONNECT programs assist business service providers, attorneys, accountants, and marketing specialists through such activities as the following:

• *Springboard* helps high-technology and biotechnology entrepreneurs to develop business strategies. Entrepreneurs are invited to make a presentation about their company to a panel consisting of a venture capitalist or private investor, accountant, corporate and patent attorneys, marketing professionals, and an executive from a successful company in the same industry. Over the last two years, this activity has assisted sixty companies, which have raised more than $10 million in seed capital.

• *The Virtual Board* is a more sophisticated program to help senior executives think through strategic issues affecting their companies. These companies have usually been in existence for a few years and have raised some form of venture or private investment capital, or have a product, but still would like advice from an informal ad hoc board of directors on specific strategic issues.

• *The CONNECT Show on UCSD-TV and CONNECTNet on the Internet* (www.connect.org/connect) provide information on new products, services, and research as well as education about business issues confronting technology-based companies. CONNECT member companies are asked to include their company information in the on-line CONNECT directory.

• *How to Start and Manage a High-Tech Company* is a ten-week continuing education course taught by experienced entrepreneurs and guest speakers. The class regularly graduates two or three new companies.

• *The UCSD CONNECT Technology Financial Forum* is for newly formed companies in search of venture capital or seed funding. The forum features approximately thirty-five companies in two categories: high tech and biotech-biomedical. Prospective business and technology plans are evaluated annually by teams of volunteer academics, business service providers, and company experts. The forum is attended by venture capitalists, investment bankers, and private investors from all over the United States. In ten years, more than three hundred local companies have participated in the forum.

Twenty-five companies that presented at the 1995 financial forum have subsequently raised a total of $261 million from venture capital, public markets, acquisition, and corporate partnerships. Twelve companies that presented at the February 1996 financial forum raised $73 million within six months.

• *The UCSD CONNECT Biotechnology/Biomedical Corporate Partnership Forum* seeks to establish strategic partnerships and collaborations between small San Diego biotechnology companies and large pharmaceutical companies. In eight years, close to two hundred companies have made presentations securing new investments. Since CONNECT started the Biotechnology Corporate Partnership Forum eight years ago, companies that have presented have raised almost $3 billion through corporate partnership arrangements. In 1997, representatives from nine of the top ten pharmaceutical companies in the world attended the corporate forum. According to the firm Recombinant Capital, companies that presented at the 1997 forum have entered into a total of thirty-four deals. The dollar value for the eighteen deals for which data are available is over $480 million.

• *The Most Innovative New Products Awards* is an event that culminates in an annual awards luncheon each December, attended by over nine hundred local executives and service providers in the high-tech and biotech markets. Each entry is reviewed by volunteer committees of business and technical people and is recognized at the event, thus providing exposure to the local business community. Four are selected as outstanding.

- *Education and networking activities.* As a company continues to grow, practical business seminars and courses featuring expert panels and speakers help provide the guidance to ensure that growth. CONNECT also presents regular events to targeted groups within the company structure, such as HR CONNECT, CFO CONNECT, and Directors' Luncheons. Annually, CONNECT sponsors about one hundred events, serving over three hundred regional high-tech companies and four hundred business service enterprises such as banks and law firms.

CONNECT represents the kind of university program that has helped define and create the future of a region. It has done this through a process that has not relied on current wisdom or expertise in narrowly defined spheres of professional practice or academic knowledge. The unique circumstances of the UCSD campus gave rise to an innovative response rather than a response of "Sorry, we can't help you, we don't have a business school." The strategy of consulting, convening, synthesizing around common goals, and building around diverse competencies exemplifies how dialogue and collaboration can give rise to creativity and innovation.

The Creative Program Development Process

The CONNECT experience suggests some general principles of group creativity that can be replicated in other environments and for other purposes.

Identify Learning Needs. The practice of continuing higher education and adult learning is dominated by a concern with "customers" and "markets," which if taken too literally can lead to a sort of knee-jerk reaction to give people what they say they want when quite possibly what they say they want and need is not easily articulated, or even misguided. The thoughtful adult educator knows how to discern from a variety of articulated wants and needs, as well as more indirect statements of concern, what the real opportunity or problem is and what sort of educational initiative is most appropriate.

The community leaders who first met with UCSD's chancellor were promoting the idea of a degree program in entrepreneurship. On further investigation, however, it became clear that what they wanted was an educational initiative that would accelerate company formation and job creation by commercializing technologies based on the growing basic research capabilities of the region. The CONNECT concept addressed this challenge head-on and thus won their support as an innovative alternative to their original idea.

Adult educators who can discern the fundamental individual and community needs potentially addressed by an educational initiative will be able to offer creative solutions. In the process, they will become *market makers* rather than *market chasers*. But to do this, they must have the intellectual wherewithal and knowledge of the environment to understand, analyze, and synthesize important themes from what is being said.

Build the Web of Talent Needed to Discover and Develop a Creative Solution to Knowledge Needs. The intellectual and interactive skills needed to penetrate what people are saying and begin to discern dominant themes and common concerns are the same skills needed to identify the diverse talent and expertise needed for a planning or advisory group. The academic developer who is not "dazzled" by one form of expertise over another is able to serve as both an interlocutor and a motivator among teams of diverse experts. The work of the planning group needs to be guided within a broad statement of goals and general assumptions. Again, in the CONNECT example, the one-on-one discussions that occurred subsequent to the original proposal to the campus resulted in some themes articulated by the convener and shared by the planning group as they developed an academic and business plan for CONNECT. The focus on high tech, the use of diverse academics and practitioners in the design and implementation of the program, and a commitment to an approach that assured knowledge gains among all the partners in the high-tech business process served as a framework within which a group of talented (and high ego-need) individuals could work collaboratively. As already noted, CONNECT now sponsors a hundred different programs and events annually, most incubated out of the creativity of its interdisciplinary, cross-professional advisory group.

Believe in the Magic of Dialogue. What makes collaboration possible is a belief in the notion that unexpected ideas and solutions grow out of genuine conversations between groups of otherwise distinct and highly specialized individuals. What makes genuine conversation possible is a commitment to a dialogic process that is based on some fundamental assumptions well articulated in Dan Yankelovich's book *The Magic of Dialogue* (in press). The book offers some guidelines on how to assure group interactions that are empowering. The focus is on relational skills rather than instrumental or transactional skills. Yankelovich offers very specific guides, including the following:

- Err on the side of including people who disagree.
- Initiate dialogue through an act of empathy.
- Minimize the level of mistrust before pursuing practical objectives.
- Keep dialogue and decision making compartmentalized.
- Focus on the common interests, not the divisive ones.
- Use specific cases to raise general issues.
- Bring forth your own assumptions before speculating on those of others.
- Focus on conflicts between value systems, not persons.
- When appropriate, express the emotions that accompany strongly held values.
- Encourage relationships in order to humanize transactions.

Expect Synergistic and Convergent Output: The Whole Is Greater Than the Sum of Its Parts. Interactions of the character described tend to be energetic, creative, and just as importantly, fun. They give rise not only to lots of creative ideas but also to suggestions on how to make them work, resources to draw on, and offers for help. In the CONNECT case, ideas just multiplied, as did offers to recruit speakers, provide financial underwriting, develop case studies, and actually teach or lecture on a pro bono basis. It became clear that the work of the group was a reward in itself because of the mutual learning that was taking place and the camaraderie that was developing.

Understand the Role of the "Synthesizer" and "Summarizer" in the Process. The role of the convener must also include an ability and a commitment to serve as a synthesizer and a "weaver" of the ideas that have been raised, the resources identified, and the roles people might play. More is involved than providing minutes of a meeting or summarizing what was discussed. Rather, the convener links together diverse inputs into what usually emerges as consensus; the convener provides specifics about priorities and next steps. This synthesis is circulated for review and comment by participants quickly, while ideas are still fresh in people's minds and enthusiasm is still high. Talented advisers respond very positively to immediate feedback that accurately reflects their input, particularly if it places it in an integrative, actionable framework.

Test the Market for a Creative Program. Once a general plan has been developed—whether it's for a sequence of courses leading to a new certificate or degree program, or for a series of seminars, events, and technical assistance activities such as CONNECT sponsors—it needs to be validated. That is, its ability to serve a need must be assessed. This can be done in a variety of ways: focus group input, support by a core group, incremental testing of programs and courses, and ability to attract key early backers, investors, supporters.

Conclusions

A thoughtfully constructed and well-facilitated design team (or creative team) can give rise to ideas, solutions, and strategies that quite different from and often more appropriate than those of the solitary problem solver or individual creative thinker. The way we have validated and assessed the value and utility of this process at UCSD CONNECT, as well as in a variety of other innovative programs for which we have become known, is many-faceted. We assess in such ways as these:

- We look at how many people or enterprises participate or enroll in the program and if there is steady growth in their participation, which is important to a fully self-supporting, nondegree-granting academic unit.
- We assess whether the program is able to attract voluntary tuition payments, corporate underwriting, sponsorships, and foundation grants.
- We look at the community indicators of how we are "putting knowledge to work": numbers of certificate program completers in continuing education, companies formed and capital raised in CONNECT, improved K–12 test scores in classes taught by our science teacher institute graduates, viewership counts and videotapes distributed by our university television station, and so on.

- We directly and indirectly measure student, corporate, and community satisfaction with content as well as faculty, academic, and peer perceptions of quality and value.
- We assess the extent to which the program content and networks of experts and beneficiaries open doors to new opportunities (often unplanned for) that match our mission and serve our communities.

The creative process is hydraulic when it works: good ideas beget more ideas; energetic, creative people draw other energetic, creative people; and financial backing increases with each creative venture. Universities, and particularly continuing education units, need to embrace new models of creativity if they are to flourish in the decades ahead. Learning how to build and utilize webs of talent—not just individual experts—is one very promising strategy.

References

Gibbons, M. *The New Production of Knowledge: The Dynamics of Science and Research in Contemporary Societies.* Thousand Oaks, Calif.: Sage, 1994.

Porter, M. E. *The Competitive Advantage of Nations.* New York: Free Press, 1998.

Sillitoe, A. *The Loneliness of the Long-Distance Runner.* New York: Plume Contemporary Fiction, 1992.

Walshok, M. L. *Knowledge Without Boundaries.* San Francisco: Jossey-Bass, 1995.

Wilson, E. O. "Consilience." *Atlantic Monthly,* April 1998, p. 56.

Yankelovich, D. *The Magic of Dialogue.* New York: Simon & Schuster (in press).

MARY LINDENSTEIN WALSHOK *is associate vice chancellor at the University of California, San Diego.*

Mastery, plasticity, a vision for the future, and a commitment to ongoing experimentation will bring forth continuing education worthy of our field's ideals.

New Vistas for Adult Education

Paul Jay Edelson, Patricia L. Malone

This volume on creativity and its implications for adult and continuing education covers considerable territory in an attempt to suggest ways in which our field can be stretched and reinvented. All of our authors took risks—with their own organizations, with the populations they served, with the greater community, with business and civic audiences. All developed and conducted nuanced and complex dialogues within their programs and among the populations served. Forms of communication varied and often included multiple modalities—discussion groups, panels, forums, and classrooms with and without walls during both the design-development process and the implementation stages.

A multidisciplinary approach to problem solving was most frequently used; there was no single individual or disciplinary area that could offer exclusive expertise. This was most evident in Mary Lindenstein Walshok's concept of *webs of talent,* through which her creative process took flight with unexpected turns that could not possibly have occurred if the traditional deference to discipline-based knowledge was followed.

Nassau Community College took a different approach to an established program and in so doing redefined the role of continuing education within the institution, which came to be viewed differently as James Polo, Louise Rotchford, and Paula Setteducati diplomatically and carefully assumed control of a program with high visibility in their school, the labor union, and the corporation. Bill Clutter of Pace University presented the story of a similar transformation in continuing education at Pace, where outreach also became a principal way of redefining the entire university with important beneficial results.

Susan Anderson redesigned a conventional learning model for parents of schoolchildren. Like Walshok, she had to address the replacement of the traditional expert in order to engender group learning. The process progressed to self-directed learning and ultimately to the development of knowledge within a context of peer learning.

The Topsfield Foundation's study circles have promoted social change through intracommunity dialogue. They present compelling evidence that highly motivated adults can successfully address important issues and work toward crafting a better future.

Clifford Baden of the Harvard Graduate School of Education used multiple evaluation tools from numerous perspectives, omitting almost no area from careful observation and evaluation. He expanded the Management of Lifelong Education program to embrace a much broader concept of a learning community, always innovating with new program modules and formats. This is truly a case study of program dynamism at its fullest.

Folkert Haanstra's vignette of the Dutch creativity centers describes a different national approach to continuing art education. Most impressive is the dedication to outcomes assessment, a growing trend in our own country. The Dutch experiment has engendered a broader view of enhancing creativity, although with mixed results. At the same time, a changing political and social climate is less encouraging for the continuation of the creativity centers.

The most important message we want to convey to our readers is the need for constant experimentation and risk taking. Without these, even the most expert practitioners will be unable to fulfill the promises implicit in lifelong learning. Yet we realize that this is far easier said than done. Even we ourselves are held back—by the desire to keep within an acceptable zone of activity, by the reassuring routine of administrative life, and at times by feelings of futility coupled with the belief that our best efforts may not succeed. Rather than rocking the boat or creating discomfort for others through requests for new projects, we oscillate between the infinite possibilities implicit in continuing education and what we actually attempt to accomplish.

The absence of a normative standard for continuing education gives this function great flexibility and strength. That is, within our individual contexts there is no reason not to try something new. We are sensitive to many influences because we inhabit "open systems" that are driven by outside demand as much as by internal and professional mandates. Simply put, continuing education can respond to opportunities others cannot see or choose not to see. Yet the loose coupling between parts is also a perpetual source of weaknesses. Because the entire idea of continuing education cannot be precisely defined, there is no single component that is intrinsic to or must be located within continuing education. The office can be told to conduct or not to conduct certain activities. Or to transfer them to other areas. Or to have the mission defined in a narrow (or broad) manner. Very often we are referred to as a "cash cow" feeding the inefficiencies of the academic system, generating funds that are to be used to offset expenses elsewhere. The fact that few of us bridle at this view suggests how accepted it is as a part of our field. What is the real purpose of continuing education? How else can we look at what we do? Are there potentially competing concepts or visions that we can employ to broaden our range of activity? And what about fostering a different understanding of our profession among our colleagues?

Developing a strategic vision for continuing education leadership is very much a function of clarifying and then defining our own set of values. If we have the ability to organize and influence the activities of our colleagues or staffs, in which directions should it be? When it comes to continuing education, do we have a notion of *plasticity* and *mastery* enabling us intellectually to reshape our practice? Do we have that desire?

In his history of adult learning in America, Kett criticized professional continuing educators as those who viewed "higher education from the boiler room rather than the bridge" (1994, p. 187). By this he meant that, lacking vision and idealism, they could not be expected to lead and thus, by necessity, must receive direction from others on which way to power the vessel. He viewed the change in continuing education philosophy in the twentieth century as going from intellectual and academic values to those of enrollment management. It is incumbent upon us to strive for a vision of adult education that truly reaches out to transform and improve society through the most generous view of educational opportunity. That entails defining the meaning of adult education as well as its mechanisms.

References

Kett, J. F. *The Pursuit of Knowledge Under Difficulties: From Self-Improvement to Adult Education in America, 1750–1990.* Stanford, Calif.: Stanford University Press, 1994.

PAUL JAY EDELSON *is dean and* PATRICIA L. MALONE *is director of corporate partnerships at the School of Professional Development, State University of New York at Stony Brook.*

INDEX

Back Issue/Subscription Order Form

Copy or detach and send to:
Jossey-Bass Inc., Publishers, 350 Sansome Street, San Francisco CA 94104-1342

Call or fax toll free!
Phone 888-378-2537 6AM-5PM PST; Fax 800-605-2665

Back issues: Please send me the following issues at $23 each.
(Important: please include series initials and issue number, such as ACE78.)

1. ACE _____

_____

_____

$ _____ Total for single issues

$ _____ Shipping charges (for single issues *only;* subscriptions are exempt
from shipping charges): Up to $30, add $5^{50} • $30^{01}–$50, add $6^{50}
$50^{01}–$75, add $7^{50} • $75^{01}–$100, add $9 • $100^{01}–$150, add $10
Over $150, call for shipping charge.

Subscriptions   Please ❑ start   ❑ renew my subscription to *New Directions
for Adult and Continuing Education* for the year 19___ at the following rate:

❑ Individual $54   ❑ Institutional $90
NOTE: Subscriptions are quarterly, and are for the calendar year only.
Subscriptions begin with the spring issue of the year indicated above.
For shipping outside the U.S., please add $25.

$ _____ Total single issues and subscriptions (CA, IN, NJ, NY and DC
residents, add sales tax for single issues. NY and DC residents must
include shipping charges when calculating sales tax. NY and Canadian
residents only, add sales tax for subscriptions.)

❑ Payment enclosed (U.S. check or money order only)
❑ VISA, MC, AmEx, Discover Card #_____ Exp. date_____

Signature _____ Day phone _____
❑ Bill me (U.S. institutional orders only. Purchase order required.)
Purchase order #_____

Name _____

Address _____

_____

_____

Phone_____ E-mail _____

For more information about Jossey-Bass Publishers, visit our Web site at:
www.josseybass.com   **PRIORITY CODE = ND1**